How to Lead

JO OWEN

How to Lead

What you actually need to DO to manage, lead and succeed

Harlow, England • London • New York • Boston • San Francisco • Toronto • Sydney • Tokyo • Singapore • Hong Kong
Seoul • Taipei • New Delhi • Cape Town • Madrid • Mexico City • Amsterdam • Munich • Paris • Milan

PEARSON EDUCATION LIMITED

Edinburgh Gate
Harlow CM20 2JE
Tel: +44 (0)1279 623623
Fax: +44 (0)1279 431059
Website: www.pearsoned.co.uk

_____

First published in Great Britain in 2005

ISBN 978-0-273-69364-2

British Library Cataloguing in Publication Data
A catalog record for this book is available from the British Library

Library of Congress Cataloging-in-Publication Data
Owen, Jo
 How to lead / Jo Owen.
    p. cm.
  Includes bibliographical references.
  ISBN 0-273-69364-6 (pbk.)
    1. Leadership. 2. Management. I. Title.

 HD55.7.O946 2005
 658.4'092—dc22

                                                                2004063514

10 9 8
09 08 07

Ten cartoon illustrations by Roger Beale, and five by Laserwords
Typeset in 9.5pt Iowan by 70
Printed and bound in Great Britain by Ashford Colour Press Ltd.

The Publisher's policy is to use paper manufactured from sustainable forests.

For the leaders of the future in Teach First and beyond

Contents

Acknowledgements

Creating this book has been a personal journey of discovery, in the course of which I have met many old and new guides to help me along the way. I would not have even started the journey without the inspiration of the staff and participants of Teach First: if they are the leaders of the future, our future is in good hands. I hope this book helps them on their journeys towards leadership. I would not have had the courage to start the book without the gentle support of my agent, Frances Kelly, and my editors, Rachael Stock and Benjamin Roberts of Pearson.

In the course of researching this book I have drawn on the time and support of many people. Monitor Group produced some refreshingly practical research for Teach First which is used in the book. I spent many hours interviewing on video a range of outstanding leaders in the public, private and voluntary sectors. My thanks to the following for giving both their time and their very practical insights: Baroness Amos, Paola Arbour, Alastair Ballantyne, Prof. David Begg, Sonia Blandford, Graham Brady MP, Dominic Casserly, Humphrey Cobbold, Steve Crawshaw, David Gold, David Gregson, Des Gunawardene, David Hanson, John Hempsey, Martina King, Nick Kitchen, Max Landsberg, Penny Lawrence, John May, Dame Judith Mayhew, David Morley, Jeremy Newsum, Prof. Nigel Nicholson, Dame Mary Richardson, Anthony Salz, Rajeev Singh-Molares, Ralph Tabberrer and Phil Willis MP.

In the course of writing this book, I have received plenty of useful feedback on the book and the programme from Teach First participants and FLAG members, including Stuart Brown, Sid Djerfi, Tom Fogden, Louise Lee, Nicola McKie, Katherine Pothecary, Pedram Prasamand, Mark Richardson, Mark Smith and Katherine Willis. My thanks to them and all the other participants who have endured the programme. The staff of Teach First have done an extraordinary job in creating such a success. On the leadership side, my particular thanks go to Susie Currie, Tia Lendo, Nat Wei and Brett Wigdortz.

Leaders, like authors, learn to take responsibility. So blame the failings of this book on me, not on the wonderful support I have received from so many current and future leaders.

Leadership skills index

Introduction

Leadership is too often shrouded in mystery. To become leaders we are urged to become a combination of Genghis Khan, Nelson Mandela, Machiavelli and Ghandi. A few people feel that they are already that good. The rest of us feel slightly small when measured against such giants.

The mystery deepens when you try to define what makes a good leader in practice. We all can recognize a good leader in our daily lives. But no leader seems to conform to a single template.

Some academics and consultants decided to solve the mystery of leadership. They had time on their hands – they were on safari. By way of a warm-up exercise they decided to design the perfect predator. Each took responsibility for one element of the predator. The result was a beast with the legs of a cheetah, the jaws of a crocodile, the hide of a rhino, the neck of a giraffe, the ears of an elephant, the tail of a scorpion and the attitude of a hippo. The beast promptly collapsed under the weight of its own improbability.

Undeterred, they turned their attention to designing the perfect leader. Their perfect leader looked like this:

▶ creative and disciplined
▶ visionary and detailed
▶ motivational and commanding
▶ directing and empowering
▶ ambitious and humble
▶ reliable and risk taking
▶ intuitive and logical
▶ intellectual and emotional
▶ coaching and controlling.

This leader also collapsed under the weight of overwhelming improbability.

66 *The good news is that we do not have*
                          to be perfect to be a leader. 99

The good news is that we do not have to be perfect to be a leader. We have to fit the situation. The polar bear is the perfect predator in the Arctic but would be useless in Papua New Guinea. Winston Churchill had to endure what he called his 'wilderness years' in peace time. He just happened to be perfect as a wartime leader. The same leader enjoyed different outcomes in different situations.

How to Lead is about becoming an *effective* leader, not the perfect leader.

In search of the pixie dust of leadership

There has been a long search for the alchemy of leadership: we all want to find the elusive pixie dust that we can sprinkle on ourselves to turn us into glittering leaders.

The research for this book sometimes felt like a search for the pixie dust of leadership. Over 700 individuals helped by identifying what they saw as effective leadership at all levels of their organizations. In addition, over 30 CEO-level individuals in the public, private and voluntary sectors in both small and large organizations gave in-depth interviews. If anyone knows about the pixie dust, they should. I also reviewed 25 years' experience of working with over 70 of the world's best, and one or two of the world's worst, organizations to see what patterns of leadership emerged. Over the past few years I have even worked with some traditional tribal groups in east and central Africa and Papua New Guinea to see how they are led.

The bad news is that there is no pixie dust. Or if there is, they are hiding it very well.

But there is plenty of good news:

▶ Everyone can be a leader. The leaders we talked to came in all sorts of flavours and styles and all had different success formulas.

▶ You can load the dice in your favour. There are some things that all leaders do well. It does not guarantee success, but it does make it more likely.

▶ You can learn to be a leader. You do not have to be someone else: you do not have to become Napoleon. You simply have to be the best of who you are.

This book shows how you can acquire the consistent characteristics of effective leadership and how you can adapt them to your own style.

Unravelling the mysteries of leadership

Leadership is inundated by small words with big meanings like *vision* and *values* and *integrity*. It is a subject which suffers from an extraordinary amount of hype and nonsense. In my exploration of leadership the mysteries began to melt away. The leaders gave reassuringly practical answers for some common questions about leadership:

▶ Can you learn to be a leader?
▶ What is this vision thing?

▶ Do values have any value in reality?

▶ How do leaders with apparent weaknesses succeed?

▶ Why do some great people fail as leaders?

▶ What do leaders look for in their followers?

▶ What makes a good leader?

▶ Is a leader just the person at the top?

▶ How do you handle conflict and crises?

What follows is not a theory of leadership. It is the collected wisdom of people who are leading at all levels in different types of organizations. The result is a book which can act as your coach to being an effective leader at any level of any organization.

❝ Your coach to being an effective leader at any level of any organization. ❞

In search of any leadership

The search for leadership started with an easy question: what is leadership? This promptly lost everyone in a jungle of conflicting views expressed both forcibly and persuasively. Everyone recognizes a good leader when they see one, but no one agrees on a common definition.

One dead end was the belief that leadership is related to seniority. Leadership is not about position: it is about what you do and how you behave. So it follows that:

▶ The person at the top of the organization may be in a leadership position, but they may not be leading. They may be careful stewards of a legacy organization.

▶ Leaders can exist at nearly all levels of the organization.

▶ Leaders need followers. You may be smarter than Einstein, but if no one is following you, you cannot be a leader.

At this point it made sense to start looking for the skills and behaviours that effective leaders have. I made a surprising discovery. Many leaders not only lack some basic management skills; they know they lack those skills. Being good at writing memos, giving presentations, accounting acumen, strategic insight or deep technical expertise is useful, but not essential. Most leaders rated intelligence as a low priority for leadership. Either they were telling the truth or they were demonstrating the humility of great leaders. Think of some familiar political or business leaders; it is clear that they are not necessarily the brightest or the best or the most competent or the most skilled in every area.

> *66 Most leaders rated intelligence as a*
> *low priority for leadership. 99*

By now I was lost in the leadership jungle. Skills seemed to be a dead end; styles of leadership could take us in nearly any direction.

It was time to look more closely at behaviours of leaders. Suddenly, a way forward opened up. People know what behaviours they expect from the leaders of their organization. The key behaviours expected of a leader at the top of the organization are:

- ability to motivate others
- vision
- honesty and integrity
- decisiveness
- ability to handle crises.

It is worth reflecting for a moment on what is not in the list: management skills, reliability, intelligence, ambition, attention to detail, planning and organization all failed to register. As this leadership journey unfolds, we will explore what these behaviours really mean and what we can do to demonstrate these behaviours effectively.

It was now tempting to declare victory. But the list did not look right. What we expect of top leaders is not necessarily the same as what we expect of emerging leaders. The 700 volunteers who helped in the search for leadership confirmed this suspicion. The behaviours they value in emerging leaders are totally different from the behaviours they expect in senior leaders, as shown in the list overleaf.

Expected behaviours of recent graduates and senior management

Recent graduate	Senior manager
Adaptability	Ability to motivate others
Self-confidence	Vision
Proactivity	Honesty and integrity
Reliability	Decisiveness
Ambition	Ability to handle crises

(Source: Teach First Survey Results, Monitor Group analysis)

There is one glaring omission from the list above. Performance. It does not get a mention. In working with leaders it is clear that they are, normally, performance obsessed. But they do not talk about it as a leadership quality: they assume that if you have the right qualities, then good performance will flow naturally from those qualities.

By now, the leadership search was in danger of becoming lost in a swamp of words and ideas. Life is already complicated enough without drowning in a swamp of leadership ideas. Fortunately, a simple map slowly began to emerge out of the swamp. All the grand words and ideas came down to a few simple principles which apply to leaders at all levels. For the sake of alliteration and simplicity, I have called them the three and a half *P*s of leadership.

Three of the *P*s dropped out of our research readily. Performance is the odd one out. If I was being intellectually rigorous, it would have no place in the leadership framework because only one of the selected leaders really focused on performance. Most leaders saw performance as a symptom, not a cause, of good leadership. For this reason, performance earns no more than half a *P* in the leadership framework.

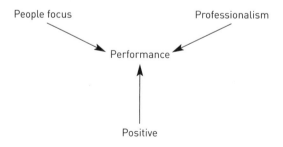

These words can mean more or less anything to anyone. So the next task was to create a more detailed picture of what lay behind these grand words and convert it into something practical that all leaders can use in their daily lives.

Creating the leadership map

Slowly, the map of the leadership journey started to unfold. Expectations of leaders across all types of organizations were clear. But expectations of leaders at different levels of each organization varied. The rules of success and survival varied. This helps explain why people often find themselves over-promoted. The rules they followed at one level do not work at the next higher level of the organization. Altitude sickness is a real challenge in leadership terms: you can succeed at one level and then simply find the challenge too great at a higher level where the rules of success have changed out of all recognition.

Too much work on leadership focuses on what happens at the top of an organization. This is a significant issue. Rules which work at the top of the organization are not relevant to someone setting out on the leadership journey. An organization full of Ghengis Khan wannabes is unlikely to be a happy place. It is no good mapping only the destination. We all need a map for the journey to the destination as well.

❝ An organization full of Ghengis Khan wannabes is unlikely to be a happy place. ❞

Managing the transition from one level of leadership to another is always a challenge. Failure rates are high even at the highest level of the organization. The career expectancy of a FTSE-100 CEO is now under five years. It pays to know how the rules of success and survival vary by level.

Eventually, a map of what good leadership looks like at each level of the organization emerged.

Much of what you can read in the effective leadership behaviours map (overleaf) may seem obvious. But before reading on, try two exercises. In the first exercise, think of some people that you rate as effective leaders at different levels of your organization and see how well they display the characteristics listed. There will certainly be some differences: as long as leaders are human there will be variation. But the chances are that, if they are good, they will show many of the characteristics to a greater degree than their peers.

Effective leadership behaviours

Effective leadership	Foundations of leadership: emerging leaders	Practice of leadership: leading from the middle	Mastering leadership: leading from the top
Focusing on people	Decentres self, manages up, supports others.	Builds commitment, good influencer. Builds networks.	Forms, aligns, motivates a leadership team.
Being positive	Has drive, ambition; is self-aware, adaptable. Finds solutions, not problems. Volunteers.	Embraces ambiguity as opportunity, not risk. Manages conflict well.	Communicates a clear vision; handles crises well; focuses on must-win battles. Decisive.
Being professional	Learns the business, learns leadership. Loyal. Reliable.	Masters core skills, sees beyond own silo.	Shows honesty, integrity; role model for core values.

There is one catch in the leadership map. When you make the transition from one level of leadership to another, the rules of the game do not change completely. You cannot substitute one set of rules for another. Instead, the rules of success are additive: you have to do all the things you did at the previous level, and then add the new rules for the new level. The leadership hurdle rises with each level of the organization.

In practice, this means that the early years of the leadership career are vital. The habits formed then will not go away. Learn the wrong habits early on, and they become very difficult to kick.

Now try looking through the other end of the telescope at some less effective managers in your organization. Reflect on why they are less effective. There are some consistent traps that leaders fall into at every level of the organization. These are not problems of gross incompetence, although those problems do exist occasionally; they are traps that decent managers easily fall into. The result is that they stay as managers and never emerge as leaders.

Ineffective leadership behaviours

Ineffective leadership	Foundations of leadership: emerging leaders	Practice of leadership: leading from the middle	Mastering leadership: leading from the top
Focusing on people	Egocentric; lives in rational world, no EQ (emotional quotient) or political awareness.	Expertise focus, not people focus; naïve about networks and politics.	Hires weak clones; threatened by talent. Delegates poorly.
Being positive	Can't do; problem focused; delegates upwards.	Retreats into comfort zone of authority, not responsibility.	Lack of stretch for self or the organization; manages a legacy.
Being professional	One of the lads or lasses.	Too political, loses trust. Leader in the locker room.	Rides the gravy train of status and entitlement.

These descriptions of effective and ineffective leaders should come as no surprise. But one more step is needed to create a useful map of our leadership journey. It is not helpful to tell people that leaders must be inspirational, or heroic, or charismatic. Most of us do not fill that mould and never will. You cannot teach or learn charisma easily. More to the point, most of the leaders felt that charisma and heroism were exactly the wrong style of leadership. Good leaders do not pretend to know it all and they do not try to do everything themselves. Leadership, for them, is a team sport. They all know they have weaknesses; their teams balance their own strengths and weaknesses.

Instead of focusing on heroism and charisma, the leaders focused on the practical skills which a leader needs. They helped to identify over 30 practical skills, which are different from the technical skills of the job (bookkeeping, legal knowledge, cutting code). They are also different in quality from the way the managers learn the same or similar skills. They are skills which the leader has to start acquiring from the start of their career.

There is plenty of good news in this skills-based approach to leadership. It blows away the mysterious guff about heroic leaders and reduces it to things that ordinary people can aspire to learn. Effective leaders do not even need to learn all the skills. All the leaders recognized that they have weaknesses and are still learning. By having the self-confidence and self-awareness to know their own weaknesses, they can build the right leadership team to help them and they could be open about continuing to learn.

Finally, all the leaders were clear that they succeeded by building on their strengths. Everyone has weaknesses – building on weakness is not a recipe for success. We do not need to try to be someone else. We simply need to be the best of who we are. We need to build on our strengths and work around our weaknesses.

This book is your guide to the leadership journey. It focuses on the many practical skills which helps distinguish effective from less effective leaders. It does not guarantee success, but it will load the dice in your favour.

« This book does not guarantee success,
                    but it will load the dice in your favour. »

PART ONE

The foundations of leadership

1

Focusing on people

The research for this book showed that what people most value in their top leaders is an ability to motivate others. But the ability to motivate others does not even register on the radar screen when looking at the qualities of emerging leaders. There is a reason for this. Most people starting out on their leadership journeys do not have anyone to manage or to motivate.

Nevertheless, the ability to focus on people is an essential early indicator of progress on the leadership journey. There are three major elements to focusing on people for emerging leaders:

1 Decentring: knowing yourself and how you affect other people.

2 Influencing people: selling ideas and the sales process.

3 Managing upwards: influencing the boss.

These are core skills which leaders at all levels of the organization have to master. Even the CEO has a chairman and a board to manage upwards; the effective CEO does not just order people to do things but also uses powers of persuasion and influence. Strong CEOs know themselves, know their weaknesses and build teams to compensate for their gaps. Stuart Rose, commenting on the strengths of retailing entrepreneur and billionaire Philip Green, said: 'He knows what he doesn't know, and not a lot of people know that.' Having the confidence to know yourself is essential for a leader.

Decentring: knowing yourself and how you affect other people

When your boss urges you to get to know yourself, smile politely and run a mile. What may follow is a barrage of psychometric testing, some psycho-babble with long words and group events where you get in touch with your inner self. At a personal level, it may be useful to check in with your inner self once in a while. For a leader, inward naval gazing is not the high road to success.

Knowing yourself is not just about looking inwards. For leaders, knowing yourself means knowing how you affect other people.

As a leader, you need to understand your own personal style and the style of the person you are working with. If you know those two things, you have a chance of knowing how to influence the other person more effectively. Some leaders seem to do this intuitively: they play people like a piano and instinctively know what tune to play to make them sing. The rest of us, who do not have this innate ability, can do some simple things to improve the odds in our favour.

❝Knowing yourself means knowing how you affect other people. ❞

There are some basic frameworks for thinking about your style and how you affect other people. One of the most popular is the Myers-Briggs Type Indicator (MB/TI). To become an expert at it takes years, which rather defeats the object of the exercise. The goal is to become a leader, not a psychological expert. MB/TI presents the leader with a series of style or type trade-offs. You can be:

- ▶ Extrovert or Introvert (E or I)
- ▶ Sensing or Intuitive (S or N)
- ▶ Thinking or Feeling (T or F)
- ▶ Judging or Perceiving (J or P).

There are also sophisticated tests to tell you which style you are: the result is normally a four letter acronym like ESTJ or INFP. As leaders, we do not have time to make everyone we meet take a sophisticated test. So look at the table below and see where you think (or feel) you come out. As you look at the positive impacts of different styles, you would only be human if you hope that you had all of these characteristics. So look at the negative impact column. This will quickly tell you what you are like and what the person you are dealing with is like. It is not sophisticated, but it is usable.

Type	Description	Positive impact	Negative impact
Extrovert (E)	Gains energy from others; speaks, then thinks	Spreads energy, enthusiasm	Loud mouth, does not include other people
Introvert (I)	Gains energy from within; thinks before speaks	Thoughtful, gives space to others	Nothing worth saying? Uneasy networker
Sensing (S)	Observes outside world; more facts, less ideas	Practical, concrete, detailed	Dull, unimaginative
Intuitive (N)	Pays attention to self, inner world, ideas	Creative, imaginative	Flighty, impractical, unrealistic
Thinking (T)	Decides with the head and logic	Logical, rational, intellectual	Cold and heartless
Feeling (F)	Listens to the heart	Empathetic, understanding	Soft-headed, fuzzy thinker, bleeding heart
Judging (J)	Organised, scheduled, tidy	High work ethic, focused and reliable	Compulsive neat freak; uptight, rigid, rule bound
Perceiving (P)	Keeps options open, opportunistic	Work–life balance, enjoys work	Lazy, messy, aimless and unreliable

Figure 1.1 Myers/Briggs Type Indicator (MB/TI) outline

Keep on using the table as you meet people, and you will quickly be able to put them in the various boxes above. Putting people in boxes works for organizational charts and burying people. But we need to do something with the information. Welcome to the style compass.

The style compass is a quick and easy way of thinking about how to influence someone. Think of someone you are trying to influence. Try to plot their characteristics on the compass, as illustrated in Figure 1.2.

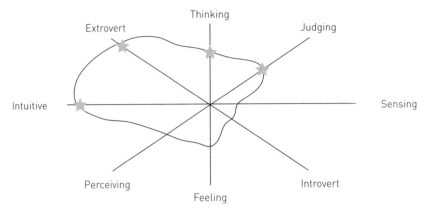

Figure 1.2 The style compass: my boss

Check this style compass against the MB/TI grid. This would imply you have a creative, extrovert boss who thinks logically, likes ideas and talks a lot. The boss is probably less excited by discussion of detail and people. Now plot yourself on the same style compass.

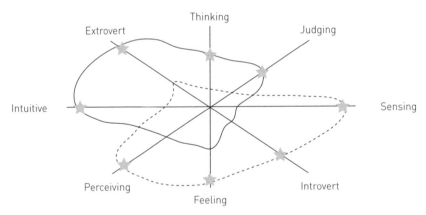

Figure 1.3 The style compass: myself and my boss

This style compass would imply that you are more or less the opposite of your boss. You think before you speak, you are more aware of people and you like practical detail. This makes you a good balance to your boss. Having people who are the same style working together sounds good but is often unproductive. Two extroverts have too much ego and too much noise for one room; two intuitive people have a thousand ideas and no action. But to get on the same wavelength as the boss, you need to adapt.

Don't bore the boss with detail and people issues, although quietly the boss will be delighted if you can take the burden of those issues away and deal with them yourself.

❝ Having people who are the same style working together sounds good but is often unproductive. ❞

The style compass is a quick way of thinking about any style, not just the sorts indicated by MB/TI. Here are a few of the other sorts of style and types indicated by other psychometric tests:

- ▶ intellectual versus instinctual
- ▶ withdrawn versus attached
- ▶ idealistic versus practical
- ▶ alert versus settled
- ▶ progressive versus conservative
- ▶ non-traditional versus traditional
- ▶ future oriented versus past oriented
- ▶ congenial versus coercive
- ▶ solicitous versus antagonistic
- ▶ receptive versus assertive
- ▶ submissive versus domineering
- ▶ acceptance-seeking versus pleasure-seeking
- ▶ sensitive versus insensitive
- ▶ socialistic versus materialistic.

Naturally, each psychometric test believes it has found the key to human nature. If you show allegiance to one of them, then the others will have you burned at the stake for heresy even as they mock your foolish ignorance. To really irritate the keepers of the psychometric faith, you can do something practical as a leader: create your own style compass. This should reflect the characteristics you think are important about the person you are trying to influence. Common themes emerge when I ask people to do this:

- ▶ big picture versus detail
- ▶ words versus numbers
- ▶ inductive versus deductive
- ▶ risk tolerant or risk averse
- ▶ controlling versus empowering
- ▶ quick versus slow
- ▶ open versus defensive
- ▶ morning versus afternoon
- ▶ positive versus cynical
- ▶ analysis versus action.

You decide what are the dominant characteristics of the person you want to influence. Map them on to a style compass, and then map where you are on the same compass. The style compass does not give you all the magic answers on how to influence the other person, but it does force you to ask the right questions about how you can adapt to get on the same wave length as the other person.

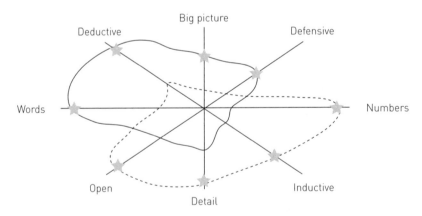

Figure 1.4   The style compass: myself and my boss (revised version)

To make it more interesting, you can populate the style compass with professions (actors, judges, plumbers, artists, engineers) to represent different styles, or with named celebrities. Most of these compasses are not printable given current libel laws.

In Figure 1.4 my boss thinks deductively; he works from the theory and the big picture downwards. I like to think I am more practical; I work from the practical detail up to the theory. He likes words and ideas; I prefer seeing the numbers and facts. He can also be a bit defensive. To get on to his wavelength I will need to adjust my style dramatically – paint the big picture of what I am proposing first, and only drive down to the practical details and numbers if he shows any interest.

You can create an endless variety of style compasses. The idea is to identify the hot buttons to press that make the other person tick. This is as much an art as a science. The important thing is the thinking process:

- What is the style of the person I want to influence?
- What is my style on the same criteria?
- What do I need to do to make our interaction productive?

Clearly, the style compass is best used when you are influencing one person. One to one is where the most effective influencing happens in practice. As soon as meetings become public, your ability to influence people is reduced. In public, people are more reluctant to commit to new ideas. Typically, people want to show that they are smart in front of their peers. The easiest way to show you are smart is to identify all the risks, problems and inconsistencies associated with someone's new idea or presentation. Smart questions are less risky than smart solutions. Once the person you are trying to influence has expressed all these doubts in public, it becomes twice as hard to make them change their mind: they would lose face in front of their peers by doing so. For these purposes, any meeting with more than two people becomes a public meeting. The third person creates the potential for any ideas and positions to be reported back into the organization grapevine in ways you may or may not recognize.

Unfortunately, you cannot rely on getting a private meeting with the person you need to influence. Sometimes, you are stuck with a public forum as the only way of communicating with the person you want to reach. In a public meeting with, say, eight people present, you have two choices.

The first choice is to be yourself. This maximizes your chances of looking confident and enthusiastic. Given that people react more strongly to visual clues and to style than they do to substance, this is important. Trying to be all things to all people is a certain recipe for failure. You will not look natural, you will not feel confident and comfortable and you will not be able to adapt to all the different styles in the room.

There is a second, subtler and more effective choice. In practice, you are probably not trying to influence all eight people equally. If the chief executive is present, it is reasonably likely that this is the person you most need to influence. If this is the case, focus the content and the style of your presentation on this person. If you are wise, you will also have quietly met some of the other people in the room beforehand and got their support in private. That leaves just the one key decision maker who you have not met. With the tacit support of the others, and the advice they may have given in private, you should be in a good position to know how to influence the CEO – you should know their hot buttons (what gets them excited), their red flags (what they dislike) and what their preferred style is. You may be in a meeting with eight people, but prepare properly and you can focus on the one person who counts most.

Influencing people

Selling ideas

Leadership involves getting other people to do things. CEOs spend a large part of their time selling their vision, selling their plan, selling their values and selling change to people inside and outside their organization. They are, in effect, salespeople. Selling is equally important lower in the organization where individuals never have enough power and authority to execute all their responsibilities. Emerging leaders are not deterred by lack of formal authority. They persuade other people to help and support them.

❝Leadership involves getting other people to do things.❞

Selling is not just about getting on the same style wavelength as the other person, although that helps greatly. You also need a process to influence people successfully and consistently. Leaders need to learn how to be salespeople.

Before we work out how to sell anything from cars to a change in your workload, we need a word of caution. Influencing people is not the same as motivating people. When you influence someone successfully, it is an event. You change their mind and they agree to something. Motivating people is more than a transaction. It is about creating a sustainable relationship. Motivated people may do things you did not ask them to do, and will do things with commitment you cannot command. We will look at motivating people in Chapter 5.

When we try to sell an idea or an object, we normally work at one of three levels:

- features
- benefits
- hopes and dreams.

Features are the easiest level to work at. Features are the innate characteristics of an idea or an object. The computer has a 3.0 GHz processor, 100 GB hard drive and 512k memory; the IT project will cost $5 million, take 18 months and will replace our existing accounting system. When people fall in love with their idea or their car, they will often spend hours boring other people with the intricate details of the idea or the car. This rarely influences other people positively.

Benefits convert the features into something that people want. So the computer may have lots of wonderful features, but the real benefit is that it can handle home video production, which uses lots of memory and processing power. At this point you may think: I would rather eat raw pigs' entrails than make a home video. So for you the benefit of the computer might be that it can handle complex engineering designs or that it can play cool video games. The point about benefits is that they are different for each person you talk to, whereas the features of the computer are the same whoever you talk to.

All this is fairly obvious. It is so obvious that people often miss it. They talk about features or benefits which are not relevant to the person they are talking to. The starting point for influencing someone is not your idea or object – it is the other person's needs and wants. If you can understand those, then you have a chance of presenting your idea in a way that is interesting and compelling to them. CEOs do this all the time. A CEO may have decided to embark on a big expansion into a new market. To sell the idea the CEO may talk about the size of the new market and its other features. But the CEO will also focus on the benefits of the idea. To the shareholders the emphasis will be on the impact on the share price. That is not a benefit to the shop floor worker. To the shop floor worker, the benefit may well be increased job security and more job variety and interest.

> **"The starting point for influencing someone is not your idea or object – it is the other person's needs and wants.""**

Beyond benefits, there are hopes and dreams. We all have hopes, dreams and fears. If you can tap into those hopes and dreams, you can influence people. One manager wanted to encourage a staff member to go on a presentation course. The staffer resisted; she felt uncomfortable doing it. Later the manager found out that the staffer was interested in amateur dramatics. He represented his idea as a way of building her stage skills, mentioning that the course would be led by an actor. The manager had related a job requirement to a hope and dream. The staffer soon became an enthusiastic and expert presenter.

As an exercise, score the next person you hear trying to sell an idea at a presentation. See how much time the person spends on features versus benefits and hopes and dreams, and see how far they try to customize those benefits and hopes and dreams for you. Low scores will probably result in your feeling unpersuaded, but a high score will probably be persuasive to you.

The sales process

By now, the main principle of influencing people should be clear: start with their agenda and style, not with your agenda and style. Read *How to Win Friends and Influence People* by Dale Carnegie. It is corny and useful in roughly equal proportions, despite being 50 years old. The core message is that you need to get on to the same wavelength as the other person. A little trust goes a long way. Going into a big sales pitch or negotiation too fast can be alienating.

What we describe below assumes that you have some degree of rapport with the other person. You have worked out their style compass and can adjust appropriately to them. The process below can be a two-minute conversation; it can be a formal pitch at a formal meeting; it can be an on/off conversation over several weeks by the coffee machine, in the car park or corridor. The point of the influencing process is to have a structured logic flow which you can follow. If you get too far ahead of yourself, you will probably find that your attempt at influencing is running into trouble, so go back to the start of the logic flow again.

A traditional seven-step sales model looks like this:

1 Agree the problem/opportunity – from the other person's perspective.
2 Preview the benefits of addressing the problem/opportunity.
3 Suggest a solution.
4 Outline how it works.
5 Pre-empt objections.
6 Reinforce the benefits.
7 Close.

We can simplify this down to three steps:

1 Agree the problem/opportunity.
2 Suggest a solution (and explain how it works).
3 Close.

Most attempts to persuade people fall at the first hurdle: failure to agree a common problem or opportunity. This is not surprising. In any organization each department has different priorities. Marketing, operations, HR and IT all see the world through different coloured glasses. The challenge for the leader and influencer is to find the common ground behind which these different constituencies can unite.

Agreeing the problem and the solution is not about talking smart. Good leaders have two ears and one mouth and use them in that proportion. In other words, listening is at least as important as talking. Listen to understand the other person's agenda, needs and wants. Then you can tailor your message to their needs.

❝ *Good leaders have two ears and one mouth and use them in that proportion.* **❞**

A good influencer tries to work out what makes the other person tick. This gets us dangerously close to the land of psychobabble. There is some argument about what really makes people tick. Here are some alternatives:

- ▶ fear, greed and sex
- ▶ fear, greed and ego
- ▶ fear, greed and idleness.

By now, you are probable spotting a pattern in these ideas: fear and greed. For the moment, we will make the implausible assumption that sex is not the basis of managerial success; someone will, for sure, write the sex-based guide to leadership. We will also take ego satisfaction as a form of greed. That leaves us with fear, greed and idleness.

Fear is a powerful motivator. If you can show that your idea will eliminate a fear ('fit our safety system and you will not die/be sued for millions of dollars'), you can influence powerfully. But the result is often compliance rather than commitment. 'Do this or you get fired' also gains compliance not commitment.

Fear is also a powerful demotivator. Humans are risk averse. Our survival instincts are well honed to see potential threats and dangers. In the managerial context, this means that most people prefer the status quo and doing nothing, rather than trying something new. So a good influencer will need to do two things:

- ▶ understand and pre-empt the objections that the other person is likely to have
- ▶ de-risk the idea.

You can de-risk an idea in many ways: pilot a project before full roll-out; phase the investment so that not everything is risked all at once; find some early wins that convince everyone your idea is a winner.

The second influencing lever is greed. This answers the question 'what's in it for me?', from the perspective of the other person. This is commonly known as the WIFM factor. Figure out the WIFM factor and you are on the way to success. Greed is not only about money. Within an organization, greed is more often about recognition by peers and bosses for a job well done and a contribution well made.

The third influencing lever is idleness. For good or poor reasons, everyone seems to feel more stressed, more pressurized and more harassed than ever before. Then along you come with a smart idea which is going to cause them more work. You will soon be told of a thousand logical reasons why your good idea is not so good after all. You need to find a way in which your idea is easy. Perhaps it fits with or supports an existing agenda of the other person. Perhaps all you need is their approval and you do the donkey work. Perhaps you can find some extra resources to get the work done for them. To overcome the natural inertia of the individual and the institution, you need to make it easy for everyone to say 'yes'.

By this point, we are still negotiating the first step of the three-step influencing process; agree the problem/opportunity.

But if you have passed the first step, you are already close to success. The second two steps are relatively straightforward.

If you have listened well, you will know what the world looks like from the other person's perspective. You can suggest your idea in a way that is compelling to them, and you should know enough to understand and pre-empt any objections they have. Remove the fear factor, remove the idleness factor. Suggesting the idea does not have to be a formal sales pitch; it can be an apparently casual conversation. The whole influencing process may take several meetings, by the vending machine as well as in offices, before you fully understand the person you are influencing.

Finally, you need to close the discussion. Weak influencers are often nervous about asking for agreement or the next steps. But the person you are influencing is unlikely to be psychic. You have to ask explicitly at the end if they agree. You have to explain the next steps. Failure to ask for agreement or the next steps means that you will have had a nice discussion and nothing will happen. You need to close the discussion by making it very clear what happens next.

There are different forms of closing – all of them lead to action:

1   The assumed close. Simply indicate what action you will take going forward. This is an assertive close. It assumes the other person is in agreement. To be sure that they really do agree, try to involve the other person in the action steps. If they do not clearly see that they are involved, they will passively accept and ignore your assumed close.

2   The action close. This is a close relation of the assumed close. You focus on the next steps but then you explicitly ask whether the other person agrees with the way forward you have outlined.

3   The alternate close. This is the sneaky but powerful close. You give the other person a choice, 'Would you prefer the premium model or the standard model?' It sounds quite reasonable and you are offering a choice. But it is a limited choice; you are not asking if they prefer to have no model at all. Disagreeing with an alternate close takes effort. Many people accept the limited choice you have given them.

4   The direct close. This is the simplest, but most dangerous, close. Ask the question: 'Do you agree to the way forward?' Like all good lawyers, you should only ask the question if you know what the answer is going to be. The direct close does invite a negative response or further discussion, unless you have prepared the ground thoroughly.

The important idea is to follow the logic of the influencing sale:

▶   Have we agreed the problem/opportunity? (Fear and greed, the WIFM factor.)

▶   Have we outlined the solution? (Pre-empt objections, reduce the fear factor, reduce the risk, overcome idleness and inertia.)

▶   Have I closed by gaining explicit agreement to the way forward?

Whenever trying a new model for the first time, it will feel awkward. Eventually, it will become second nature.

Managing upwards: influencing the boss

All the leaders who took part in the research for this book recognized the importance of managing upwards. It is a career necessity. It is also a very good way of learning core skills. Because we have no authority over our boss, by definition we have to learn some highly effective influencing skills to succeed. If we can influence our boss, we should be able to influence anyone. Because the boss tends to be around a lot, we also get a lot of practice in trying our influencing skills. It can, naturally, be a very frustrating experience.

Managing the boss is a vital leadership development exercise. The reality is that our boss is more important to us than we are to the boss. It is an unequal relationship. Because of this, we all tend to spend a lot of time figuring out how to succeed with the boss. In effect, we are actively developing all the influencing and management skills which we need to succeed. The boss makes a very good guinea pig for this exercise. We can see the effects of our efforts nearly every day, and we can try a variety of different tactics and styles.

On the other side of the coin, the boss expects to be managed. Even CEOs want their direct reports to manage the relationship effectively.

In this section we will look at two alternative perspectives on managing upwards:

1 What bosses look for in emerging leaders.
2 How you can influence your boss successfully.

What bosses look for in emerging leaders

The 700 leaders who took part in the research for this book showed what they expect, in general, from emerging leaders:

▶ adaptability
▶ self-confidence
▶ proactivity
▶ reliability
▶ ambition.

By themselves, these words can mean more or less anything. We will look in more detail at what these words really mean in later chapters.

To make the research interviews more interesting, the leaders were asked if there were any fatal mistakes that emerging leaders could make. Reassuringly, most leaders appeared to be reasonably forgiving and tolerant. They accepted that emerging talent makes mistakes; they accepted that new talent would not change the world immediately and that they would find it difficult adjusting to a new world of work.

They all identified one unforgivable sin: disloyalty.

❝ Many sins are forgivable, but disloyalty is not one of them. ❞

Many sins are forgivable, but disloyalty is not one of them. To be disloyal is to break the fundamental basis of trust on which any team has to operate. The boss has to be able to trust the team and also has to be able to earn their trust in return; loyalty and trust is a two-way street. Disloyalty can be expressed by gossiping negatively about the boss, failing to support fully some unpopular or necessary decision, or following a separate agenda. In the words of one rather defensive boss, 'Don't outshine me, don't outsmart me and don't outflank me'. In other words, disloyalty is not a case of plotting the downfall of the boss. It is a failure to act as a fully committed member of the team.

Naturally, your organization will have plenty of formal evaluation criteria around things like teamwork, initiative and problem solving. Whatever the formal criteria are, if you are totally loyal and committed to your boss, you will probably find that the formal evaluation will be made to look good as well. It is difficult for bosses to be hard on people who have tried hard and been totally loyal. Of course, if you have a gold medal in incompetence then nothing will save you.

How you can influence your boss successfully

Influencing the boss has three elements:

1 Finding the right boss.
2 Delivering the right results.
3 Having the right behaviours.

Received wisdom is that bosses manage and staff are managed. This is, potentially, a recipe for hell on earth. If you have a good boss, you are lucky and will enjoy the relationship. If you have a bad boss, you are in trouble. Most of the leaders I interviewed said that they could identify emerging leaders at an early stage in their careers. They could see individuals with leadership potential: the real indicator of likely future success was the boss they worked for. If they worked for a good boss, they were likely to learn effective skills and behaviours. If they worked for a bad boss, they picked up all the wrong skills and behaviours. Picking the right boss is essential from a very early stage.

Depending on the luck of the assignment process is not a good way to manage the leadership journey. It becomes less of a climb to the top and more of a random walk through the foothills and swamps of management.

Finding the right boss

Emerging leaders need to manage their careers, and they need to manage their bosses.

You may get lucky and stumble across the right boss for you. But you might also get unlucky. You will not just have an unpleasant time with the wrong boss. You will also pick up all the wrong leadership behaviours from the wrong boss. Many people are happy to play the lottery on the vital assignment process. When you enter a company for the first time, you do not have much choice. In practice, there are a couple of things you can do to load the dice in your favour:

▶ Find a sponsor, or sponsors, in the organization who are senior to your immediate boss. Make yourself useful to them. They are likely to return the compliment when it comes to assignment time and can help guide you to the better assignments and bosses.

▶ Work the assignment process. People tend to know which are the death-wish jobs and bosses. When those jobs and bosses are looking for staff, it makes sense to assume the cloak of invisibility or extreme work overload – either way, you are mysteriously unavailable. Volunteering to do some work for your delighted sponsor is a good avoidance strategy. Conversely, when a good boss is looking for staff it does no harm at all to let them know how excited you would be about working with them on that assignment.

If this looks unduly political, then welcome to the world of work. Political skills count.

This assumes that you are managing your career within one organization. However, there will come a time when you want to look beyond your current organization. Be careful: the grass always looks greener on the other side of the fence. The reality is that bosses come and go, just as your assignments come and go. So even if you have a lousy boss, you need to think how permanent that situation is likely to be. Moving jobs, like suicide, often turns out to be a permanent solution to a temporary problem. And, like suicide, you cannot be sure what the future holds once you have made your move.

You are in a better position to judge opportunities and bosses within your current organization than you will be in a new organization. When you move organizations, you inevitably find that you have to start all over again in building networks of support and trust, finding out how things work and finding the right boss and the right assignment. Even if you think you have found the ideal boss in another organization, you need to think how long that person is likely to stay your boss.

Despite the caution over moving to find the right boss, there is an alternative perspective. For most people, *career* is a noun. It describes how they move steadily through an organization. For some of us, *career* is a verb which describes how we move from triumph to disaster in different and unexpected ways across companies and countries. Careering can be a lot more fun than having a career.

Delivering the right results

Influencing the boss is a matter of both style and substance. Style has been dealt with at some length above. You should be able to draw a reasonably accurate style compass for your boss, understand its implications and act on it.

Style without substance may be good for C-list celebrities, and even for some B- and A-list celebrities. It is not a good recipe for leadership success. You need to be able to deliver the right results. The question is: 'What are the *right* results?'

Sometimes the right results are pretty obvious. If you are a bond dealer or any sort of salesperson, you will have clear and explicit targets. More often, there is a degree of ambiguity about what you are really meant to achieve. The vagueness of the formal evaluation criteria (teamwork? judgement?) does not help.

The formally correct answer is to sit down with your boss and have an expectations exchange. Discuss openly and candidly what is really expected on both sides. You may get a partial answer at best. If you do not yet know each other, it is difficult to know what both sides can and should expect. Moreover, not all bosses are comfortable being open and honest about expectations.

In practice, you have to work out for yourself what is really expected. You have to become an expert at reading the smoke signals from the office of the boss. You have to figure out what the boss's agenda looks like. There are probably a couple of big things that the boss needs to achieve in the year, and then there is an awful lot of other stuff that has to be dealt with. You can help either by taking away some of the 'other stuff' so that the boss can focus more attention on the must-win battles. Or you can help directly by removing road blocks and accelerating progress towards the must-win battles. The recipe for failure is dragging the boss into spending too much effort on the 'other stuff' or failing to recognize the importance of the must-win battles.

Having the right behaviours

Different bosses have different styles. You have to adapt to their behaviour because they will not adapt to yours.

> ❝❝Ideally, the relationship with the boss is a partnership.❞❞

Ideally, the relationship with the boss is a partnership. It may be an unequal partnership but you still have to play your part. At the heart of the successful relationship are clear expectations. Your boss should delegate to you not just the 'administrivia' and messy tasks on the basis that shit rolls downhill. Effective delegation also gives you projects which play to your strengths. You need to help your boss know what to delegate and how much. You need to make sure your boss understands three things at all times:

▶ What you are good at. The boss cannot play to your strengths if you do not know them yourself. Some people are good at analysis, or dealing with people, or selling, or organization; different projects suit each type of strength.

- What your capacity is. In the professional world, it is very hard to estimate workloads accurately. There is too much ambiguity about the size of the job. Bosses have a simple way of dealing with this; they keep loading work on you until you scream. If you work at home all night, that is your problem. Manage expectations. Let them know when you have spare capacity (volunteer for work) and when you are at capacity. The easy way of doing this is to ask the boss what the priorities are for your assignments. This is an easy way of saying you cannot do everything.

▶ What your progress is. Bosses hate surprises. If you are ill, they need to know enough so that they can arrange cover.

These are all simple disciplines which are routinely ignored. The result is that people get the wrong assignments, work too hard, have crises and underperform. They then complain about their boss, showing they are disloyal and soon find themselves on the leadership exit ramp over the cliff edge.

Emerging leaders do not blame their bosses. They take control and influence the boss as far as they reasonably can.

2

Being positive

Look at what the surveyed 700 leaders said they looked for in emerging leaders:

- adaptability
- self-confidence
- proactivity
- reliability
- ambition.

Much of what they are looking for can be summarized in one idea: being positive. We live in a cynical age. The media daily bring news of wars, disasters, corruption and crises. In any organization it is easy to see many things that are wrong: unreasonable and demanding bosses and customers, shoddy service, confusing organization and endless petty and not so petty demands. These failings are often discussed at length, around the coffee machine. It is sometimes hard to rise above such cynicism.

The surveyed CEOs were all fundamentally positive. They believed they could change and improve things. Where other people saw problems, they could see opportunities. Even conflicts would be accepted as an opportunity to learn and grow. None of the interviewed senior executives was cynical about what they were doing or about their organization. Perhaps cynical leaders do exist in some organizations. Whether you would want to work for them is another matter.

> **❝ Being positive is a fundamental requirement for leadership. ❞**

Cynicism is something that can be indulged in among junior staff who intend to stay that way: cynical and junior. Being positive is a fundamental requirement for leadership. Before progressing further it is worth thinking about what being positive is and is not about:

Being positive is about:

- ▶ seeing opportunities, not problems
- ▶ learning to be lucky consistently
- ▶ moving from analysis to action
- ▶ living better.

Being positive is *not* about:

- ▶ happy clappy happiness and saying 'Have a nice day' through gritted teeth
- ▶ false optimism
- ▶ false praise and 'one-minute-managing' people
- ▶ ignoring problems, risks and realities
- ▶ hoping for the best and gambling.

Being positive can be learned. To accelerate the process of discovering the positive world we will look at five aspects of being positive:

1 Shrinks and the art of being positive in everyday life.
2 Leaders and the art of being positive in business life.
3 Leaders and the art of being consistently lucky.
4 Being smart versus being positive.
5 Problem solving positively.

Shrinks and the art of being positive in everyday life

If economics is the dismal art, then psychology is perhaps the dismal science. It spends most of its time looking at why we are all messed up.

But not all psychology is dismal. Martin Seligman, a professor at the University of Pennsylvania, was elected President of the American Psychological Association in 1996. He proceeded to stun his membership by pointing out that focusing on illness all the time was missing an important point. If we could focus on wellness and help people stay well, then many psychological problems would either not occur or would disappear: prevention is better than cure. He realized that shrinks needed to pay more attention to people who were well and find out why.

Seligman's message is important for leaders. The journey to leadership is a marathon, not a sprint. Many people drop out not because they lack the skills or aptitude, they drop out on the way because they burn out. The initial enthusiasm of the career – the pizza-fuelled late nights working to meet deadlines – begins to wear off. Sustaining the career takes stamina. Even now, the research on how to achieve these goals is incomplete. Perhaps it never will be complete. But there are some core lessons about how to sustain being positive:

▶ Focus on strengths, not weaknesses. This is essential for all leaders; you cannot succeed by dealing with weaknesses. Successful leaders play to their strengths: they focus on tasks where they can make a positive difference. They also find tasks for staff that allow staff to shine and compensate for their own weaknesses.

▶ Manage your feelings. If you feel upset or angry, that is your problem, not that of the person who has caused you to feel that way. At all times you have a choice: you can feel angry, upset or bored; or you can feel engaged and interested. If you want rain showers in your soul, that is your decision; if you want sunshine in your soul, that is your decision too. Leaders learn to wear the mask of leadership: whatever they may feel inside, they are able to project the face that they want to project.

▶ Visualize: sportspeople always try to visualize success. When they focus and concentrate enough on this, they shut out the outside world. Focus on the goal, and then on how to get there. Our surveyed leaders could all articulate in simple words what they wanted their organizations to achieve.

▶ Do something worthwhile, which may or may not be in work. It could be family, friends or philanthropy. If you are not doing something worthwhile, it may be time to look elsewhere. Not everyone can or wants to become a leader. If you prefer to go fishing, leadership will not help you.

▶ Move to action. Do not pick over the past. Look to the future and take control of it. Most of the leaders we met had experienced crises or failures. Most of them did not see it quite that way – they saw each experience as a chance to learn, grow and become stronger. There was no victim mentality of looking at the past and blaming others for misfortune; they looked to the future and took responsibility for themselves.

All of this is mind-numbingly obvious stuff, but very hard to see when in the heat of battle or depths of depression. There are more sophisticated versions of positive psychology promoted by Seligman, Csikszentmihalyi and others. Reading academically intense work about being positive can be hard work and depressing. Seligman's list of 24 Positive Values in Action (VIA) becomes a mountain in the way of becoming positive. I will spare you the full list. Leaders do not have time to become shrinks. We need something simpler, personal and usable. Welcome to the peace of mind chart.

Date:	30/6	14/7	21/7	4/8	18/8	1/9	15/9
My organization is worth working for.	3	3	3	3	3	3	3
I have worthwhile goals.	1	1	3	3	5	5	5
My boss supports me and my career.	2	3	4	4	5	5	5
I am in control of my work and destiny.	2	2	3	4	4	4	4
I have the skills and resources to succeed.	4	4	3	3	3	2	2
I am recognized for what I do.	2	2	3	3	3	4	4
I balance work and personal lives.	2	2	4	5	2	3	2
Total	16	17	23	25	25	26	25

Figure 2.1 My peace of mind

It is easy enough to create your own peace of mind chart. The more specific it is to you, the better. Record the state of personal relations or activities; soon you will see which ones mean most to you. As you look at how you feel about different things, you can decide where you want to take control, change things and move forward. Intuitively, everyone keeps personal score of their own peace of mind. The peace of mind chart simply makes explicit what is implicit.

Leaders and the art of being positive in business life

Leaders always seem to be able to be positive. At the heroic level, the words of Churchill still echo down the ages: 'We will fight them on the beaches… ', 'their finest hour…'. No one remembers him saying, 'We're in deep shit.' He could find the positive and focus on action. He could also express it very well.

At a slightly less heroic level, business leaders see opportunities where others see problems. Akio Morita, the founder of Sony, visited New York. He saw gangs of youths with boom boxes on their shoulders blasting out music. Most people saw and heard pure nuisance. He saw that young people wanted music which they could take with them. The idea of the Sony Walkman was born in his head, and a few billion dollars later the problem had become a landmark success.

The leaders interviewed also had the same positive outlook on more or less everything. They even viewed conflict as being positive – it is a way of sorting out priorities within the organization, and it is a way of learning more about yourself and the other person.

There are some consistent ways in which the emerging leader can demonstrate a positive outlook:

▶ Bring solutions and opportunities to the table, not problems.
▶ Respond to new ideas by looking for the positives, not the negatives, of the ideas. Most junior executives try to prove they are smart by finding all the risks and problems, not by exploring the opportunities.

- ▶ Volunteer for special projects. Smart emerging leaders volunteer early so that they get a project which suits their strengths rather than waiting and then finding they are assigned the project from hell.

- ▶ Take measured risks. You will always be forgiven for doing your best and going the extra yard, even if you fall over in the process. You learn more and earn more respect from trying to go the extra yard than by playing it safe.

There are also some 'don'ts' when it comes to looking positive:

- ▶ Don't whine about the menial work you have to do. It's a rite of passage. Get over it. It's in the menial work that you often learn the most valuable lessons about how the organization really works.

- ▶ Don't gossip about your boss and colleagues. Word gets round and it damages the reputation of the gossiper.

- ▶ Don't duck responsibility. It is very obvious to bosses who goes the extra yard and who does not.

66 *Being positive pays for a leader.* 99

Being positive pays for a leader. One CEO has a unique reputation in the fierce and aggressive world of investment banking – no one has ever heard him say an ill word about any colleague or competitor. The result is that he is universally trusted and liked. Anyone who has a conversation with him knows that they are not at risk of being bad-mouthed behind their backs. Because he is so positive, he is a leader that easily acquires followers. Nor does he duck the tough decisions that have to be made, especially in investment banking. If a unit is not succeeding, he will cut it back, not because the people are failing but because the market is weak. If an executive is failing, it is because the executive is in the wrong position, not because the executive is lousy.

Being positive is a discipline that can be learned. Learn not to complain or gossip or point out negatives; volunteer for stuff; bring solutions not problems to the table. Occasionally, try smiling. These are all disciplines that can be acquired and eventually they become second nature.

Being cynical and negative, pointing out problems and risks, is an easy way to show that you are smart. Being positive involves more risk, but in the longer term people who are positive command greater respect than people who are negative.

Perhaps the finest name ever created for a company is 'I Will Not Complain'. It was founded by professional adventurer Anthony Willoughby. He found that if only one person in a group started complaining, it was corrosive to the morale of the entire group. In all subsequent expeditions, members had to sign a pledge promising: 'I will not complain if I am eaten by tigers or if porters are used to carry beer not food'. People stopped complaining, and morale kept high. Occasionally someone might observe (at –25 degrees centigrade) 'It's very cold', which would then provoke a debate about whether that was a complaint or an observation.

Leaders and the art of being consistently lucky

When the surveyed leaders were asked if they had been lucky, they all said that they had enjoyed lucky breaks. Then they would quickly add, 'but you have to make your own luck'. They were somewhat like Napoleon, who liked lucky generals until he met Wellington and Blucher. In other words, there is more to luck than the spin of the roulette wheel. You can be consistently lucky or unlucky – it is up to you.

At the risk of drowning in a deluge of alliterative Ps, luck normally boils down to three principle Ps:

1 Practice
2 Persistence
3 Perspective

Practice

'The harder I practice, the luckier I get' has been attributed to both Gary Player and Arnold Palmer. Both of them lived the quotation. With practice, the 20% chance of a holed putt becomes 30%, the 30% chance becomes a 40% chance and so on. The lucky putt is in effect the skilled putt.

All the CEOs surveyed had considerable experience of their sector, be it in law, consulting, investment banking, voluntary service, education, retail, consumer goods or politics. None had successfully led in multiple sectors. Perhaps I was not looking hard enough because there are individuals who arise from one experience and suddenly find themselves becoming chairman of multiple companies, voluntary organizations and public commissions. They find themselves leading everything, from their dog to the future of the nation.

But there is a difference between the leaders with in-depth knowledge of their sector who effect real change and the leaders who have the status of being chairman of commissions and committees. The chairmen are often in leadership positions, but they are rarely leading: they are empty vessels that look important and make more noise than progress. This is confirmed by Jim Collins in his book *Good to Great*, which found that the CEOs who made the biggest difference to shareholder value and company performance were not the media darlings who got all the headlines. They were the leaders who quietly built their businesses based on deep knowledge and experience of their sector.

Experience is to the leader what practice is to the sportsperson. Experience enables the leader to identify patterns, spot opportunities, make the connections between new technology and existing customers, and see trends early enough to act on them. The leader who hops from sector to sector has none of these advantages.

The CEOs emphasized the importance of experience. They do not expect emerging leaders to change the world early in their careers. What they expect is that emerging leaders will develop a keen understanding of the organization and the sector, and perhaps bring a fresh perspective to challenge established norms.

Persistence

The difference between success and failure is often no more than a matter of giving up or carrying on. In the film industry stars often become an overnight success after 10 or 20 years of trying.

Richard Wiseman, a professor at Hertfordshire University, has made a study of luck. In his book *The Luck Factor* he describes a housewife who is always winning competitions, on average three or more a week. This is astounding good luck which has brought her free cars, free holidays and free money. Her luck is perhaps more understandable if you know that she enters about 60 competitions a week. This is serious effort. Naturally, the more competitions she enters, the better she gets at competing. Practice and persistence often go hand in hand.

In the United States it is more or less a badge of honour for an entrepreneur to have had at least one bankruptcy in the past. The leaders interviewed could all recount crises in their careers when everything went wrong. Failure is a natural part of leadership: if you have never failed, you have probably never tried hard enough. An emerging leader will need to take measured risks and push to the limits. Without doing this it is difficult to learn what you can and cannot do.

The test of a leader is how they react to failure. Giving up, getting depressed and feeling cheated or let down by other people are not good reactions. Learning positively from the mistakes made and moving forward to the next challenge are better reactions. In Chapter 6 we will look in more detail at how leaders deal with conflict and crises.

Perspective

'The harder I look, the more I find' could be the summary of perspective. Lucky people often find themselves in the right place at the right time. Lucky people know that they are in the right place at the right time because they have been looking for it. Unlucky people probably do not even know that they are in the right place at the right time. One leader talked of being offered a very exciting position by the chairman of HSBC. The first time it was offered, she did not realize it was being offered to her. She had prepared herself for a different conversation in which she had to defend her organization against loss of sponsorship. She was the right person in the right place at the right time but she could not see it. She was working on the wrong agenda. Only when someone else pointed out what was happening did she realize her mistake. She was able to get a second chance and made no mistake.

Leaders have to be able to see the opportunities that are in front of them. Virgin Atlantic started out as a successor to the low-cost and ill-fated

Laker Airlines. It had a tiny upper-class area which could take about 12 people in the upstairs section of the old 747s. The service in upper class was far better than anything else its rivals provided, if only because it was small and it existed to satisfy the whims of Virgin's owner Richard Branson and his music industry friends. Soon enough, the popularity of upper class spread. Branson had the wit to realize that success would not come from cheap economy tickets, but from great service to attract the premium-fare customers. So he changed the business model from cheap and cheerful to a premium price and service model. He succeeded; Laker failed.

At the other end of the scale, Michael O'Leary found himself CEO of a one-aircraft Irish airline which was going bankrupt. Twelve years later the airline, Ryanair, is larger than British Airways in market capitalization. O'Leary simply imported the no-frills, low-cost, deep discount airline model from North America. The model had been succeeding in full view of everyone. O'Leary was the first to see it and import it.

This perspective does not come from a random process of looking around the world. All the leaders interviewed have a deep knowledge of both their own organization and the industry in which it operates. They are always looking and learning more about themselves and their peer group. The harder they look, the more they find.

Around us there are endless examples of people who have created businesses which now seem so obvious that we could have done it. The internet has spawned online book selling (Amazon), betting (betfair.com), travel (lastminute.com) and computers direct to the public (Dell). These are obvious now; at the time they were not obvious to most people. Least of all were they obvious to the traditional booksellers, bookies, travel agencies and computer makers. They were all looking in the wrong direction – at their traditional way of doing business and at their traditional rivals. It is one thing to see an opportunity; it is another to act on it. There is no such thing as a good idea which has not happened. With perspective, you need courage to start, as much as you need courage to persist when things go wrong.

Being smart versus being positive

Smart people often fall into the trap of being clever. This is not a good idea for leaders. Unfortunately, smart people are very good at seeing what is wrong, seeing problems, seeing risks. They see how the dumb boss is always messing up. They ooze superiority and cynicism.

As a simple rule, emerging leaders respond to challenges with one of the four *A*s:

1 Apathy

2 Analysis

3 Answers

4 Action

The apathetic are never going to become leaders and are unlikely to remain employees for long. The problem for smart people starts with the analysis response. A typical staff response to a proposal is to identify risks, challenge data, question assumptions and highlight problems. It shows that the staff person is diligent, thorough and clever. But it simply gives everyone else more problems to deal with.

The potential leader will bring not just a problem to the table, but will also suggest a solution. This involves the risk of being wrong. That is a risk that all leaders have to learn to deal with. And most leaders are very forgiving of people who try to bring solutions, not just problems, into their office. At least you are trying to make their life easier.

The most courageous response is to move to action. There is an informal rule in most organizations that 'it is easier to ask forgiveness than it is to ask for permission'. Leaders are prepared to take calculated risks and move to action when working through the formal machinery of the organization would take too long. Whatever the outcome of the action you take, you should benefit.

If you succeed, you should gain recognition. If at first you fail, you probably have enough initiative and drive to get help, try again and find a way of succeeding. Most bosses are delighted to back and help anyone who is trying to take a problem off their plate. Failure in its own right can be a very useful, if painful, learning experience. Those who sit quietly on the sidelines taking no risks learn nothing.

Smart people often try to find the perfect answer through analysis. Leaders will find an answer that works through a combination of experience and experiment: they move to action fast and recognize that the perfect answer is often the enemy of the practical answer.

Problem solving positively

Problem solving is at the heart of both management and leadership. Problem solving is not just an intellectual exercise. Effective problem solving drives to action. This makes it a political and practical exercise as well. Decisiveness came high in the leaders' list of expected characteristics of an effective leader. In many ways, decisiveness is a better word than problem solving. In the academic world, it is possible to do great problem solving which results in zero action. In the business world, problem solving has to lead to decisions and to action. Unlike the academic world, the business world never waits for the perfect solution. The perfect solution takes too long to find. The perfect is the enemy of the practical.

The standard requirement for business problem solving is to have too little time and too much ambiguous data to solve the problem. This makes problem solving more interesting.

Most problem solving approaches are solid. They recommend a thorough, structured approach which ensures that you will not fail. At best, you might get B+. To get an A* grade, you need more than a thorough, structured analysis. You need some insight. Telling people to be insightful is like telling them to be intelligent. It does not really help them. So we will not look only at how to be structured and thorough. We will also look at how you can raise your chances of at least appearing to be insightful.

The structured and mechanical approach to problem solving looks like this:

1 Find the problem.
2 Create a hypothesis.

3 Create a data structure.

4 Find the data.

5 Review and analyze the data.

6 Make a recommendation:

The more insightful approach looks like this:

1 Find the problem and the owner of the problem. Challenge the stated problem: is it a cause or a symptom? Why is it a problem?

2 Create a hypothesis. Find an alternative perspective and approach; talk to people.

3 Create a data structure. Challenge the data and the definitions. Find alternatives.

4 Find the data. Look widely for insights and killer facts, then quickly narrow the search. Do not boil the ocean.

5 Review and analyze the data. Build a story based on the hypothesis; do not be neutral. If the story does not work, create another hypothesis which works better.

6 Make a recommendation. Pre-sell the solution and recommendation to all the interested parties. Identify and resolve concerns before the recommendation becomes public.

Most problem-solving guides focus on solving the problem. This is rational and unhelpful. In practice, the time spent on problem solving often looks more like this:

▶ Defining the problem and the approach: 20% of the time.

▶ Finding data, researching and analyzing: 50% of the time.

▶ Pre-selling and refining the solution: 30% of the time.

Solving the problem is half the effort, at most. Investing time in defining the problem or selling the solution is rarely wasted. They are as important as solving the problem itself.

Below, we will look at the different approaches.

Find the problem

If you can find the problem, the solution is often quite easy. Even CEOs find it easy to latch on to the wrong problem, and hence the wrong solution, very quickly. The right answer to the wrong problem is still going to be wrong in the end. Invest time at the start to make sure you are heading in the right direction.

Three traps await the unwary:

1 Problem-free solutions
2 Problem-free analysis
3 Focus on causes, not symptoms

Problem-free solutions

This is the most common trap for leaders. In its simplest form the snake oil salesman calls on the leader with the latest version of corporate snake oil: supply chain management, core competences, acquisitions, re-engineering, whatever. And there are the testimonials to show that the snake oil genuinely transforms businesses. No leader dares be left behind: if everyone else transforms their businesses, doing nothing is not an option. The snake oil salesman makes another sale.

> **❝ Selling umbrellas is fine if it is raining, not if your customer is going scuba diving. ❞**

The snake oil salesman is a solution in search of a problem. Selling umbrellas is fine if it is raining, not if your customer is going scuba diving. When you hear a solution, your first reactions should be:

▶ What is the problem this solves?

▶ Is this our most important problem?

You will soon find out if the solution is relevant or not. As in exams, it pays to know what the exam question is.

Problem-free analysis

I once did (what I thought was) a brilliant analysis on a company. I presented (I thought) brilliantly to the board. At the end the CEO coughed quietly. He thanked me. He then paused and said: 'I only have one question. What, exactly, was the problem you were analyzing?'

I promptly evaporated in a mist of vanity and confusion. Always know what the problem is you are analyzing. Most importantly, know whose problem it is. If it is your problem, keep it to yourself. If it belongs to someone else, make sure that you are analyzing the problem they want you to solve.

Focus on causes, not symptoms

Challenge the stated problem. Treating the spots on a child's face won't help if the child has measles. Get to the cause of the problem. A common business problem is to complain that costs are too high; the solution is to cut costs. I was asked to help the back office of an investment bank in Japan to cut costs. This seemed odd, because the business was growing fast. Cutting people, property and infrastructure is an interesting way to grow. After many discussions their problem became clear: unit costs (productivity) were poor. This meant that growth was unprofitable. They wanted to grow in total, but they wanted to keep costs and headcount down. They needed to raise the capacity of the existing infrastructure, not cut it. The two problems are totally different. The cost-cutting approach would have led to firing people (expensive for a Tokyo-based client); the capacity-raising approach retained the people but with better systems and processes.

Create a hypothesis

If you know what the problem is, you can probably create some hypotheses about the solution. The hypothesis is vital so that you keep focused on the outcomes and so that you can focus the analysis. There is not time to boil the ocean of facts in the hope of finding every last drop of information. Good hypotheses help achieve focus.

There are two ways of creating a hypothesis. The easiest way is to talk to people. Ask lots of people in different areas for their views. People are rarely short of opinions and are normally flattered to be asked for them. Inevitably, each opinion is biased. As you hear the people speak, you will probably hear the sound of axes being ground.

The second way is to structure the problem so that it can be split up into bite-sized chunks of analysis and potential insight. This is outlined below.

Create a data structure

This is the staple of problem solving. There are two principles at work here:

1 The 80/20 rule

2 The issue tree

The 80/20 rule

The 80/20 rule is a non-scientific assumption that 80% of the results can be achieved with 20% of the effort. This may be an underestimate. What-ever the ratio really is, it implies that you should prioritize your efforts. Focus the data search on those areas which are most likely to yield results. Once you have seen what those results look like, then you can decide if and where to focus further effort. Do not try to do everything; there is never enough time.

You can turn the 80/20 rule around. In terms of time management, 80% of your effort is spent achieving 20% of the results. Leaders need to time manage ruthlessly: delegate away the time sinks and focus on the few things that make the biggest difference. You will also find 20% of your staff consume 80% of your time, 20% of your customers produce 80% of your profit and 20% of this book produces 80% of the value to you. The trick is to know which is the 20% that counts.

Here are some issues which often help decide which is the 80% and which is the 20% in problem solving:

▶ impact on organization

▶ importance to owner of the problem

▶ feasibility of potential solution

▶ ease of analysis

▶ cost of analysis and potential solution.

The issue tree

They say that the best way to eat an elephant is one mouthful at a time. It is perhaps better not to eat elephants at all. However, if you are faced with a complex problem, the same principles apply. If you have to do it, break it down into manageable, bite-sized chunks. Once you have identified the bite-sized chunks, you can apply the 80/20 rule to decide which parts of the analysis are most worthwhile to attack first.

A simplified example of an issue tree is in the figure below. It looks at how an organization might increase profitability. If only life was as simple as this issue tree, but at least it gives a structure and a focus to the problem-solving effort.

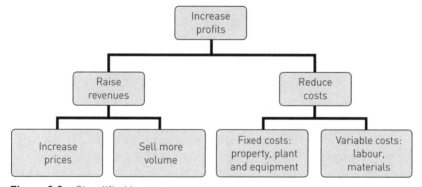

Figure 2.2   Simplified issue tree

Find the data

Information is rapidly becoming a commodity, but insight remains as precious as ever. The process of finding good data is relatively straightforward for anyone who is familiar with the sources and the industry. A good analysis will look for original cuts of information. Use market research on a product or service, but even more usefully, film it in use to show how it is really experienced. Find the killer facts and data. Often the drama and emotional impact of a film or a killer fact far outweigh reams of turgid market research tables. Once you have the right answer, use information like a lawyer, not a detective – to support a case rather than find the truth. Examples of killer facts I have found and used include the following:

▶ A utility thought it already had a highly demanding performance culture. But it emerged that staff were 72 times more likely to die in service than to suffer performance sanctions: top companies like GE and IBM annually cull the bottom 10% of performers.

▶ An insurance company believed it was becoming flatter and more empowering: we identified 12 layers of management in an organization of 1500 people. There were three levels of executive dining room. We argued, slightly provocatively, that one billion Catholics make do with just five levels of management (on Earth) from pope to people: pope, cardinals, bishops, priests and people.

Case*Study* **B+ versus A* grade problem solving in action: the conglomerate**

This was an assignment I took on as a newly minted MBA: the mechanical analysis I did produced a textbook answer which was very precisely wrong. Luckily, I had a partner who had a brain and insight instead of an MBA and a textbook. He got to the right answer.

Problem. Which of our portfolio of businesses should the client build up, sell or close?

B+ approach. I did a thorough portfolio analysis. I used standard business school grids: BCG grid; cash use/generation and competitive position/market attractiveness grids. These gave the standard answers: milk the cash-generating but low-growth businesses. Invest in some of the strong, high-growth businesses. Good theory, bad practice.

A* approach. The senior partner looked at the analysis and ignored the results. I thought he was insane. He focused on where the company added value and had expertise relative to other companies. It was strong in the boring but cash-generating low-growth business: it could buy up rival businesses on the cheap and turn them round. It could fund the acquisitions by selling some of the high-growth businesses. Because all the competitors were doing the same B+ analysis, they were selling the low-growth businesses on the cheap and were prepared to buy the high-growth businesses for a fortune.

Summary. The A* approach recommendation is the opposite of the B+:
A*: buy low-growth businesses at low cost; sell high-growth at high price.
B+: sell low-growth businesses at low cost; buy high-growth at high cost.

The A* approach succeeded because it built on the company's strengths, not on abstract business theory. The company bought up many orphan brands at low cost from large companies and used its expertise to maintain and build the intrinsic value of the brands.

Killer facts are not a substitute for the hard grind of analysis. They bring drama and conviction to analysis, which another 100 pages of research are unlikely to achieve.

Case*Study* **B+ versus A* grade problem solving in action: the electronics retailer**

By the time I did this case, I had learned that mechanical answers get mechanical results; you need to look a little harder to get insight.

Problem. The client wanted to know what its customers really wanted: low prices, convenience, service, expertise, product range etc.

B+ approach. The client had truckloads of consumer research: attitude studies and tracking studies and benchmarking. Customers, not surprisingly, told researchers they preferred low prices to high prices. Duh. So the client built up a low-price strategy.

A* approach. We challenged the data. Attitudes are biased. After the event people will rationalize their choice and give you the answer they think they ought to give. No one likes to think they paid over the odds. So we researched what people did, not what they thought. We caught shoppers as they left shops and asked them how much they had spent (if anything), how many shops they had been to and what they were looking for. It became clear that shoppers were totally confused by the choice: they could not make meaningful comparisons across all the features, brands, warranty and financing options. After getting confused, they would buy from anyone who was helpful and gave them a reason to buy: they wanted a story to tell their neighbours they had been smart ('I got free delivery/double memory/a larger screen/a 10% discount' – any story would do).

Summary. The B+ approach led to cost cutting, price wars and no profit. The A* approach led to price reassurance (advertising special deals) but to a higher overall price/service/profit offering. We looked for an alternative perspective on the data by looking at behaviour, not attitudes.

Review and analyze the data

The intellectually pure way to review data is to search the data for anything which might disprove the initial hypothesis. Then you revise the hypothesis in the light of the new information until you have a hypothesis which stands up to the highest levels of intellectual scrutiny. This may well succeed in a university. It does not succeed in a business.

There is an easier way: tell a story.

> **"** *If you have created a good hypothesis, you should be able to construct a simple story to make your point.* **"**

We are all natural storytellers, and we all tend to remember stories. Try to remember a few stories, and then try to remember a few business documents. Stories, for most people, tend to be more memorable. If you have created a good hypothesis, you should be able to construct a simple story to make your point. Here are two stories I have told:

1 To an overcentralized retailer. They did everything in house: their own printing, design, advertising, label manufacture, research. They were so self-contained, war could have broken out and they would not have noticed. We had mountains of value analysis to show how inefficient this was. They were not impressed. So we took the board on a walk round the medieval centre of their home city. We had a professor from the local university talk about how the city only started to prosper when it focused on one or two major activities for which it became famous across the land. It stopped trying to do everything within the city walls; it started to trade instead. When we got back to the board room they recognized they had become like the medieval walled city. They needed to start to focus, and they decided to start outsourcing non-core functions for the first time.

2 To an internally focused utility company. We filmed an elderly lady whose home had been flooded with sewage. The water company had responded slowly and ineffectively; the film of the lady in distress brought reams of dry market research to life. Similarly, we filmed the experience of checking in for an airline, and the customer experience of trying to set up a computer. These visual stories are not substitutes for research, but they provide drama and emotional engagement which a PowerPoint presentation will not achieve.

Telling a story needs a little creativity. But the result is that all the dry analysis has to be focused around a simple, memorable message. Once this happens, it becomes easy to sort out all the verbiage and excess analysis. The effort of doing analysis makes many people want to present it all: it is their way of showing that they have done a good job. Ultimately, leaders are not rewarded for working long and hard – they are rewarded for working well. So put the excess analysis into an impressive appendix and focus the recommendation on the story.

Make a recommendation

By the time you make a recommendation, there should be no surprises. To anyone. If you are surprised by someone objecting to your recommendation, you have failed. The process of pre-selling an idea to all the interested parties helps improve both the quality of the analysis and the quality of the outcome.

The quality of analysis is helped by talking to all the interested parties from an early stage. If they disagree with the way that your hypotheses or analyses are going, you can get early feedback. You can then amend your hypothesis, do further analysis, or find a way of incorporating their ideas into your recommendation. Politically, it makes sense to pre-sell the recommendation. It is far better to have disagreements in private. People tend to be more honest in private. Once they have taken a public position, it becomes difficult for them to back down without looking weak; they tend to reinforce their initial position, and a disagreement can quickly escalate into full-scale warfare.

The process of consensus building is time consuming and frustrating. But ultimately, you are not meant just to solve a problem: you have to make something happen. You need enough consensus that there will be action. If one constituency is very threatened by what you recommend and resists, despite your pre-selling, at least you will know the nature of the opposition and you will have built up enough support to help the organization move forward.

Remember that leaders tend to evaluate the quality of information and recommendations two ways. They will look closely at the logic of what is before them. If they are good, they will know the core statistics for the organization by heart; if there is a doubtful number they will challenge it.

One bad number destroys the credibility of the entire presentation. Check and double check all data. Validate each piece of data with a relevant constituency. If there is financial data, make sure that the financial people will stand up for the data if it is challenged; make sure marketing will stand up for any marketing data you present.

“One bad number destroys the credibility of the entire presentation. ”

The second way that leaders evaluate recommendations is on the reputation of the person presenting. Each person is like a brand who has differing levels of trust and quality. If you are unknown, or untrusted, expect some scepticism. Enlist the support of people who are trusted either to present or validate the recommendation.

3

Being professional

Professionalism encompasses the core skills and values that define the character and potential of the organization and the individual. It is central to the success of leadership. It means different things at different levels of leadership.

For the leaders at the top of an organization, professionalism is fundamentally about the values that they display. Some leaders fail this basic test. They get to the top of the organization and promptly put their snouts in the trough of perks, privilege and pay. The worst ones go to jail, the others simply serve to undermine morale within their organization and undermine respect for business in the wider community. Other leaders set an example and live the values of the organization. Professionalism can never be taken for granted.

In the middle of an organization, professionalism is about mastering core skills. In theory, we all know how to read, write, talk and listen. In practice, a few months in most major organizations will raise doubts about everyone else's ability to do these things. We write well but others never seem to read our golden prose; we suffer the deluge of tedious, poorly written reports and e-mails which show others cannot write; we endure tedious presentations by self-important speakers who fill the air with little more than their egos and yet no one listens properly to our own brilliant presentations. In

Chapter 7 we will unravel the mystery of why we can read, write, talk and listen in a social context but fail dismally in a managerial context.

For the emerging leaders professionalism has four elements:

1 Learning to learn leadership.
2 Learning the local rules of the game: understanding professionalism in the context of the organization.
3 Learning some universal lessons of professionalism.
4 Learning business survival etiquette.

These professional capabilities are cumulative: the lessons learned as an emerging leader have to be carried forward and added to the professional skills of the leader in the middle. The leader at the top has to add a final set of professional values to the values and skills that have been picked up on the way to the top.

Learning to learn leadership

Let's start with the good news: it is possible to learn leadership. If you know how to learn leadership, you are well on the way to success.

❝ It is possible to learn leadership. If you know how to learn leadership, you are well on the way to success. ❞

The bad news is that neither the education system nor corporate training systems develop leaders. The formal education system teaches people exactly the wrong lessons about leadership, which may help explain why so many successful leaders, like Richard Branson and Bill Gates, dropped out of education prematurely.

The education system teaches people to work in a highly structured environment, where individuals work largely alone to find a logical answer. Any potential leader who hopes for a structured, predictable environment where there is a logical answer and in which they can work alone is likely to be deeply disappointed.

Corporate training sessions do not help much either. They can, like business schools, do a fine job of transferring a body of knowledge about accounting or operations or finance. But leadership is not about technical knowledge alone. Leadership requires enabling people to achieve things.

Corporate training tends to focus on explicit knowledge: technical skills which can be embodied in books, e-learning and courses. This is the knowledge that the West has focused on with great success. Tacit knowledge is more about know-how than about know-what – it is the elusive knowledge about how to do things well. Much of the Japanese tradition, which has served them well in manufacturing and quality, has been about tacit knowledge. Corporate training which tries to focus on tacit knowledge often subsides into tree hugging, raft building and abseiling. Some people like it, but few leaders develop from it. No leaders we talked to pointed to any training courses as the essence of their success.

In practice, leadership is not about explicit knowledge that goes into books and courses. It is about tacit knowledge; books only help the process of structured observation and discovery that help leaders find the leadership style which works best for them.

Leaders typically develop their capabilities in two and a half ways:

1 Learning from role models: learning from leaders.
2 Learning from experience: career as a noun and a verb.
2½ Learning from structured observation and discovery (sometimes).

Learning from role models: learning from leaders

Everyone learns from role models. Within an organization, your role models are successful peers and, for better or worse, your boss. This learning process can be quite unconscious. David Begg, the head of Tanaka Business School, recalls hearing someone give his own lecture, with his own mannerisms and his own phrases. It was like looking in a mirror. He was, in fact, watching his very first mentor from whom he had unconsciously copied much of his own successful style of lecturing. It is important to find the right role models and to learn the right lessons from them: pick up the wrong habits from the wrong role model early in a career, and it becomes very hard to change course.

HOW TO LEAD

As individuals we all create our own leadership DNA; we steal a bit from one leader and a bit more from another leader we admire. Equally, we use a little leadership gene therapy to get rid of unhelpful DNA; seeing a colleague mess up is a very valuable lesson about what not to do. By stealing lots of DNA from lots of sources we land up becoming unique. In turn, other people steal bits of our DNA. Thankfully, we never clone each other completely. In one consulting firm we had a water cooler game of 'spot the mannerism': we could identify certain mannerisms that different partners had and we could trace it back to one or two people that they all admired. Leadership skills are infectious. As with all infections, we do not realize that we are either infecting anyone or that we are being infected in turn.

For the most part, the process of learning starts out unconsciously. Emerging leaders see some people blow up and do their best to avoid the same fate. They see some bosses do really smart things and will try to incorporate that into how they operate. At an early stage, emerging leaders quickly absorb the rules of success and failure in their chosen organization. Many find that the rules of the game are not to their liking and will venture off to another organization in search of a game where they can do better.

Copying role models is particularly useful in conflict, crises and difficult situations. Asking the question 'What would X (who I admire greatly) do in this situation?' often creates clarity where there was fog and fear. Try it next time you face a challenge.

For many people, learning leadership in this way is a random walk; you bump into good role models and bad ones alike. This puts the emerging leader at the mercy of luck. Get a good boss and role model and you learn all the right habits. Get a poor boss and you get lousy learning which takes a long time to unlearn. There are obvious career management implications here: get the right boss. There are also implications for making learning leadership a more structured and productive exercise. These implications are spelled out below.

Learning from experience: career as a noun and a verb

The second way that leaders learn is from personal experiences, triumphs and disasters. They gain this experience in two different ways. As noted previously, some leaders gain experience through a structured career; others gain it by careering through different experiences in a more unstructured way.

Leaders who have had a career (noun) build up a deep knowledge of their industry and organization. Some corporate organizations, like Unilever and GE, actively move their younger talent around the world and around businesses and functions so that they can build the breadth of experience to become effective leaders.

For other leaders, *career* is a verb which describes how they have moved from one experience to another in different sorts of organizations. In a less structured way than the large corporate organization, they too have built a breadth of experience which enables them to become leaders.

Whether *career* is a verb or a noun, existing leaders emphasise the importance of getting the right experience and the right role models early. Taking risks at the start of a career is easier than taking risks later on – a 26-year-old can start over again more easily than a 46-year-old. Many 26-year-olds recover from a false career start by the simple expedient of doing an MBA.

Smart people often fail as leaders because they chose the wrong experience at the start of their careers. The bags of gold being offered by banks and professional services firms are attractive to anyone with student debts. But sitting in front of a screen for three years trading bonds or preparing presentations prepares no one for leadership. Less glamorous careers where you learn to deal with people, not computers, are often a better grounding for future leadership.

Learning from structured observation and discovery

Learning from experience and role models is not hugely attractive to a generation which wants it all and wants it now. Listening to the older generation advising them to settle down for the long haul and wait their turn which may, or may not, come along in 25 years is not inspiring to a 25-year-old.

There are two ways of accelerating the path to leadership.

The first is to go out and set up your own organization. The learning will happen very fast. Even if the enterprise fails, you will have learned a lot. It can be an expensive way to learn.

The alternative way of accelerating leadership learning is by structured observation and discovery. Do not leave the learning to a random process of osmosis, which depends on getting some good role model bosses and good experiences. You might land up with some lousy role models and have some lousy experiences.

Instead, structure your learning from experience and from role models by using this book. You cannot read a book from page 1 and finish it at page 200 as a leader. But you can use this book to accelerate your discovery process by knowing what to look for. Throughout the book, there will be opportunities to look at what others do and at what you do and to decide what works best for you. There is no universal leadership formula: there is only what works for you and the people you work with.

❝ You can use this book to accelerate your discovery process by knowing what to look for. ❞

Experience suggests that people largely ignore worksheets in books such as this. So we will save your time and the planet's trees by not printing lots of structured observation worksheets. Instead, you can create your own customized worksheets to help you reflect on how peers and bosses either do things well or less well. If you force yourself to observe and reflect on what is working and what is not working, you will quickly build up your own preferred operating style, which will be far better than some theoretically perfect technique described in a book.

To help you on your way, the list overleaf gives you 30 headings to start thinking about and observing. In each case, the goal is to find an example of someone who you thought did it well or poorly and figure out why you thought they did it well or poorly.

Do not be constrained by the headings in the list. Many of the things you observe will not fit into any obvious category. As we talked to leaders about the role models they admired, we picked up things which are often too subtle to be placed in any one category, for instance:

- ▶ 'Our chairman never said a bad word about anyone, ever. As a result, we all trusted him, we knew we would not be bad-mouthed behind our backs.'

- ▶ 'The head of products was decisive because he was focused. If you asked him for a decision on a marginal issue, he would decide instantly. If it was not part of his central agenda and the decision was finely balanced anyway, he figured that you might as well toss a coin.'

- ▶ 'My boss helped when I was struggling. He did not tell me I was failing. He said he thought I was potentially great and could not understand what was holding me back. He asked for my ideas. I talked, he listened and by the end I left with total confidence that I and he knew what we needed to do to succeed.'

- ▶ 'I used to get angry and would lose my temper. Then I realized, like road rage, it achieved nothing. I still get angry, but I cannot remember when I last lost my temper. I just assume the mask of leadership and ask myself, "How would a good leader act now?" I then calm down and act much better with the mask on.'

Over time, you will assemble a list of insights that work for you. In the course of this book you will discover some of the things that have worked for other leaders in the areas listed below. What works for others is not an answer for you, but it is a starting point on the journey to discovering how to make the best of who you are.

Interpersonal skills
Setting goals and expectations
Giving informal performance
   feedback (good and bad)
Giving a formal assessment
Motivating
Managing and resolving conflict
Giving praise and recognition

Communication skills
Presentations
Listening
Effective e-mails
Effective reports
Handling bad news
Interviewing skills

Management skills
Meeting management
Problem solving
Negotiation
Networking
Upwards management
Problem solving
Time management
Decision making
Vision
Team management
Project management
Delegation
Crisis management

Personal behaviours
Courtesy and etiquette
Empathy
Enthusiasm
Stamina
Risk taking and management

Leaders who learn ... and leaders who don't

Teaching leaders to lead is perverse. Senior leaders have 20 or more years of experience that demonstrates that they are successful individuals. They do not take kindly to clever people coming along with some new theory that implies they do not know how to lead. But most of the CEOs we spoke to readily admitted that they have weaknesses and that they are still learning. Some are quite blunt about it: 'I'm crap at some things', said one.

Senior leaders learn the same way as emerging leaders – from experience and from other role models. Inevitably, there are a few leaders who think they have all the answers and can learn nothing from anyone. They are often larger than life characters with larger than life egos. They often provide useful lessons to emerging leaders on how not to lead.

Learning the local rules of the game

Every organization has a set of rules which are not written down but are ignored at your peril. In some cases, the rules are plain confusing. When it comes to dress codes, an increasing number of organizations are totally schizophrenic. A large IT services company wants to look professional to its customers, so the dress code is fairly conservative suits and ties in the client marketplace. But it wants to appear funky, high-tech and youthful in the recruiting marketplace, so internally the dress code is very much dress down. In advertising agencies the client side and the creative side dress totally differently. Senior staff dress differently from junior staff. Dress codes are an elaborate way of declaring tribal loyalty and caste status. With the advent of dress-down days, they are also a useful indicator of the economy: in good times people dress down, in bad times they dress up.

Dress codes are a trivial but highly visible sign of the need to understand the local rules of the game. Understanding the rules becomes more important when it comes to matters such as taking risks and taking initiative. In the dealing room of an investment bank, risk taking is the life blood of the organization. In the Civil Service it would be a nightmare for all the staff to be taking risks with the policies of and procedures of the government.

The challenge is to learn the rules of the game fast. Even experienced leaders trip up on this. They hear the siren calls of the headhunter who lures them away to apparently greener pastures to work for a competitor. In theory, it should be easy. They know the industry and they know the job. But they do not know the culture of the new organization; they do not have a network of support and alliances; they have no internal track record and they do not know which levers to pull to make things happen. When the headhunter promises greener pastures elsewhere, remember that it is greenest where it rains most.

> **❝When the headhunter promises greener pastures elsewhere, remember that it is greenest where it rains most.❞**

In theory, it should be possible to ask about the rules of the game. In practice, no one will tell you. It is a bit like asking people how they breathe; even if they knew the answer, they would still think it a pretty weird question. You have to pick up some clues and hints. At minimum, sit down with the boss early on and ask what his or her expectations are and what a good outcome in six months' time looks like. You might also ask how you can really mess up. One boss who had hired me to be a salesman said the worst thing I could do would be to sell anything. This was, to put it mildly, surprising. I asked what I should do. 'Make yourself useful' he said, unhelpfully. So I did: I left and set up a bank instead. It helps to get misunderstandings and bad bosses out of the way early.

The simplest way to find out the rules of the game is to look at people who are seen to be successful in the organization – people who get promotions and bonuses. See how they dress, act, talk and work.

Learning some universal lessons of professionalism

The view from the top

The top leaders interviewed in the course of writing this book were very clear about what they expected from emerging leaders:

1 Loyalty
2 Honesty
3 Reliability
4 Solutions
5 Energy

These five characteristics are closely linked. As you read through these characteristics they may strike you as obvious and simple – who on earth would be disloyal, dishonest, unreliable, problem focused and slothful? Viewed from the top of the organization, the answer is: too many people. These are very common traps. This is great news for the emerging leader. It means that you do not heroically have to change the world single handedly before you get noticed. You just have to do some very basic things thoroughly and well.

66 *This is great news for the emerging leader. You just have to do some very basic things thoroughly and well.* **99**

Loyalty

By far the most important of these characteristics is loyalty. Most leaders are forgiving of most things. As noted earlier, disloyalty is the one unforgivable sin; some leaders allow a second chance, but many will not.

In theory, loyalty should be a two-way street: loyalty should be mutual. If you perform, your boss will help you succeed. In practice, the relationship is very uneven. You can hurt their career; they can kill yours. In its worst form, the loyalty pledge is used by control freak managers to keep followers tightly in line. If the control freak delivers on commitments to help you gain the right experience, the right assignments and the right promotion, you are lucky. Sometimes they simply block your career by controlling you and not developing you. At that point you either have to escape the boss and look for another organization or break the loyalty rule and find another boss in the same organization.

Honesty

For leaders, honesty is closely connected to loyalty. Honesty does not mean 'politician's honesty' where you are honest as long as you are not caught red-handed, lying through your teeth. Honesty means being open with the facts, especially when they are awkward facts about setbacks. Bosses hate surprises; it makes them look like they are not in control and not competent. If they know the awkward facts, at least you give them a chance to help you find a solution.

Reliability

If honesty is about having the courage to be open with awkward facts, reliability is about avoiding the need to deal with the awkward facts in the first place. As one leader put it: 'Never bullshit me. Don't overpromise. If you can do something, say so. If you say you can do it, do it. If you must, underpromise and overdeliver. Never overpromise and underdeliver.' A critical part of reliability is learning to say 'no' to unreasonable requests and setting expectations right from the start. It is better to have one tough conversation about expectations before a project starts than to have three months of trying and failing to deliver the impossible. This is a lesson that effective leaders at all levels of the organization understand intimately, especially when it is time to set and agree budgets.

Solutions

Some people bring problems, other people bring solutions. The curse of smart people is that they can see all the problems, they can see all the risks of any course of action and they can see how the boss is messing up. They ooze superiority and cynicism. Then they fail. Leaders do not succeed by proving they are smart. They succeed at least in part in seeing solutions, driving to action and getting results. This takes more courage than analyzing and finding problems. It often means messing up, falling flat on your face and enduring the snide remarks of smarter people who predicted your fall. The difference is that you will learn more, achieve more and go further than the people who are smarter and less courageous.

Energy

Energy incorporates a lot of values that leaders look for: stamina, commitment, resilience, optimism, adaptability and a can-do spirit. These are positive words. In practice it means that the emerging leader is given a lot of crap to deal with and is expected to get on with it without complaining.

It is common for the newly minted MBA in a bank or consulting firm to figure out that despite their high salary, they are being paid less per hour than the partner's secretary. This is a fair reflection of their relative value to the firm. It also reflects the reality that the marginal cost of a consultant or banker is close to zero – for a few free pizzas they can be kept working all night for no extra salary.

The sweatshop approach to learning the business is not pretty. But all the leaders we talked to had an intimate knowledge of their business. The owner of a chain of 650 shops not only knew all the area managers, he also knew by name and face most of the shop managers and their staff. He has driven several hundred thousand miles around the country over 40 years building his knowledge of the business.

The view from the bottom

Professionalism is not just about impressing the boss. It also means acquiring a set of behaviours which make it easy for peers and teams to work with you. These are behaviours that become more important the more senior a leader becomes. In doing 360-degree reviews with emerging leaders, there are a few consistent complaints that people make about their colleagues. As I do these reviews, I find that everyone tends to share the same view, with the one exception of the person who is irritating all his or her colleagues. They are damaging themselves and their reputations without realizing it. The following complaints come from an exceptionally good organization. In other organizations, similar comments are typical but the intensity with which they are voiced is much greater. In rough order of priority, the comments are:

▶ Not communicating. Staff like to know what the boss is doing and why. Equally, the boss likes to know what staff are doing. It is very hard in a professional organization to manage capacity: are people overworked or not? Work is often open ended and ambiguous. Regularly letting the boss know where you are helps with capacity planning (not overloading, but giving opportunities when you can take them); it helps as an early warning system for problems; it helps with disaster recovery. If you fall ill with stress, at least it should be clear how to pick up the pieces.

▶ Public, not private, arguments. This can be as simple as one off-guard comment, something like 'this group is the best we have', which then is sure to demotivate all the other groups. In its worst form, it involves public abuse.

▶ Game playing and politicking. Everyone knows who the politicians are. They play one side off against another and use half truths to confuse things and get their way. They succeed in the short term but kill their credibility in the long term.

▶ Bullying. This is as simple as delegating badly and late. The 'hospital pass' delegation is to receive a project too late and when it fails, you get the blame. A near variation is to delegate all the rubbish and convert staff into administrative assistants. Effective delegation means delegating projects, as well as some rubbish, which will allow emerging leaders to learn and grow.

▶ Bad habits. This can be anything from turning up late to poor dress. Everyone else knows it. Make yourself approachable so that you are not left in the dark about how your habits affect other people.

▶ Personalising feedback and conflicts. The ensuing sulks help no one and achieve nothing.

The challenge for the leader is how to deal with this sort of behaviour. There is a natural inclination to fight fire with fire. But joining the unprofessionals in the gutter is not the route to the top, although it may help you achieve one or two promotions in middle management. Arch politicians who play games and bully are not playing a sustainable game. They trust no one. Equally, no one trusts them. Everyone knows that they are likely to get hurt by one of the politicians. Having no one to trust makes it more or less impossible to survive in middle management, where you need networks of support and mutual obligation in order to achieve anything.

> **&&**Having no one to trust makes it more or less
> impossible to survive in middle management. **&&**

Recognizing that the political rats are doomed to failure in the long term may be gratifying, but it does not help anyone in the short term when they are on the receiving end of such unprofessionalism.

Ignoring unprofessionalism is as ineffective as fighting fire with fire. By ignoring the misbehaviour you encourage it to continue. They know they can get away with it, so they will continue.

In theory, the correct response comes from the game of Prisoner's Dilemma, as described in the box below. The successful strategy is tit for tat: do not attack, but do retaliate. The other side slowly learns that cooperating with you is better than attacking you. This is fine in theory, but difficult in practice. In practice, a gradual process of escalation works best.

Prisoner's Dilemma

This is a popular version of game theory. It was first developed by Flood and Dresher in 1950 for the Rand Corporation, looking into strategies for nuclear war. Nuclear war disproves the old adage, 'It's not the winning, it's the taking part that counts'.

The same issues of conflict and cooperation apply to the workplace, with somewhat less catastrophic results.

In the game two suspects are locked in separate cells. They are offered four options:

▶ Admit to the crime, shop your partner and get off free if your partner has not shopped you in the meantime.

▶ Admit to the crime, shop your partner who also shops you: you both get a reduced sentence of three years for cooperation.

▶ Say nothing and get five years (if your accomplice shops you).

▶ Say nothing and get one year on a minor charge (if your accomplice also says nothing to shop you; your accomplice will also get one year).

> There are many variations of this. Rationally, you are better off shopping each other unless you trust each other, in which case it makes sense to cooperate and say nothing. If the game is played once, there is no chance to test the strategy of the other person. If the game is played many times, then the two partners can evolve a successful strategy.
>
> In the long run, the typical best strategy is tit for tat. When the other side opts for conflict, you follow. Otherwise, you default to cooperation. If you never offer conflict, you will be treated like a doormat to freedom by the other suspect: they will always shop you. If you always conflict, then both sides will always get convicted, albeit on a reduced sentence. If you slowly learn cooperation, you both get away with a minor charge.
>
> The same dynamic works in business. The cheats can succeed in the short term (which can last years). It pays to stand up to them so that slowly they can learn the price of conflict versus cooperation.

There are a few principles behind managing the escalation process:

- Give the rat repeated chances to back down and change behaviour.
- Escalate slowly, and try to manage the conflict in private and in person.
- Seek advice from mentors and allies: understand if you have a personal issue or if the rat is a rat to everyone. If it is a personal issue, deal with it as a personal issue.
- Use the boss as a last resort: they hate to deal with this sort of messy, political issue where the facts and the resolution are uncertain.

An escalating game of tit for tat in the corporate world might look like this:

1 Rat says something inappropriate: ignore it. It might have been someone under stress, a genuine error.
2 Rat repeats the offence: talk, in private to rat. Rat may sulk. Offer olive branch to rat the next day in the hope that rat has got over sulk.
3 Rat continues sulk, raises stakes with another offence: talk again in private. Summarize discussion in private e-mail to rat (start leaving the electronic paper trail). Seek advice from mentor (start testing political waters to see if rat behaves badly to all or just to you). Offer olive branch again next day.

4   Rat tries sticking knife in: talk in private again. Summarize in private e-mail again. Review with mentor again. Probably raise issue with your boss informally. Again offer olive branch next day.

5   Rat continues irrationally and offensively: take advice from mentor (again). Raise the issue formally with boss. Bosses hate this sort of issue. It is always messy. No one agrees the facts. It lands up in 'I said he said' arguments. And there is no easy resolution. Both sides get hurt by such escalation: mud sticks to the innocent as well as the guilty. The boss really wants people to sort these issues out between themselves. You need to be able to give the boss an easy-ish resolution, which is as specific and actionable as possible.

Learning business survival etiquette

Leaders do not have to have great etiquette, but it helps. With some notable exceptions, etiquette tends to improve the further up the organization people go. At the bottom, there is often low awareness of what is acceptable and what is not. In the middle, people are jostling so hard for position that courtesy gets shoved to one side. At the top, people have the time and space for grace.

So why bother until you get to the top?

Etiquette is fundamentally about putting the other person at ease and making them feel valued, respected and important. Poor etiquette fails on all these counts. Think about it. Who would you rather deal with: someone who feels at ease, valued and respected or someone who is feeling uncomfortable, defensive and devalued? Many people, sadly, would answer the latter. Powerful buyers have been known to make suppliers dance for their amusement; job applicants are often put under great stress. Little power makes little people into little tyrants. They may enjoy abusing interviewees and suppliers, but it does little to help the business.

Emerging leaders need a network of support and trust. They need followers, peers and bosses who value and respect them. Poor etiquette simply makes it harder to gain respect; good etiquette helps gain respect.

Clearly, etiquette varies from country to country and from company to company. Japan, for example, has very formal rituals for meeting people for the first time:

▶ offer meishi (name card) with both hands and bow

▶ read meishi: the name card really gives guidance to who should have bowed first, longest and deepest depending on level, location, company etc.

If this seems difficult for a non-Japanese business person to do, think how hard British etiquette is. One senior Japanese businessman finally plucked up the courage to ask me how to shake hands. Duh. It's so obvious, isn't it? Until you try to explain it: how and on what occasions, how do you signal that you want to shake hands, how do you know when the other person wants to shake, how hard do you press and for how long? Bowing is simple by comparison.

So let's look at some fairly basic etiquette which is routinely missed.

Promptness

This is not just about respecting the other person's time, although that is important. It is also about using time well. The best salesperson I know routinely prepares and leaves for important meetings early; if the plane or train is delayed or the travel instructions are ambiguous, he will still be early. As a result, when he travels he is always focused on his final meeting preparations; he is never late or stressed or unfocused on arrival. He gets through fewer meetings, but he is very good at them. Another salesperson I know is charming but routinely late. She spends the first 15 minutes apologizing and catching up on the meeting's progress. Sometimes her charm seduces clients. Other times, although the client smiles when she leaves, we are later told never to send her back again. You do not lose clients or friends being early, but you can lose them being late.

Focus

Good leaders, even at the top, have the habit of making you feel that you are the most important thing in their lives at that moment. They focus completely on you. This can be unnerving but is also effective leadership. They really are focused and they really do make the other person feel important. Good leaders assure focus in some simple ways:

- no interruptions from calls
- mobile phone off
- no playing with PDAs in the meeting.

A good way to show that you think other people are really unimportant is to check your PDA often to see if there are any interesting blogs by yodelling accordion players or to answer your phone on the off chance that someone might be able to teach your hamster yoga.

Courtesy

'Thank you' is not a difficult phrase. Try it. After I joined a new partnership, I unexpectedly found that the secretarial group was being very helpful to me at all times. I asked what was going on. They told me that at the annual partners' conference, I had been the only one of a thousand partners who had gone to their lair to thank them for all the thankless work they had been putting in behind the scenes. People like to be praised, and it costs very little to do.

Responsiveness

Answering the phone inside three rings, replying to e-mails fast and following up on commitments promptly looks like you are in control and it also minimizes effort. Slow response often leads to confusion and re-work: do it once, do it right. Of course, if there are people you really do not want to be harassed by, then not answering is the best way forward.

The personal touch

In the high-tech world, it pays to be high touch. There are many ways of adding the personal touch. A few examples:

- Try walking with your guest back to the lobby or lift when they depart, instead of having them escorted by a secretary. This can be a 'Columbo moment' (after the TV detective in a dirty mac). As he was leaving, Columbo would turn and ask one innocent but devastating question: the suspect, who would have relaxed, would blurt out the truth unintentionally. In the same way, after a formal meeting or interview, you often get to the truth as your guest relaxes on the way out. In any event, they will feel appreciated.

▶ E-mail is just another of the hundred irritations every day; a hand-written note in an old-fashioned envelope commands attention.

▶ Learn names and use them back. The sweetest word in the language is someone's own name. They not only respond, they are grateful you took the trouble to remember. If you are stuck for conversation, remember few people can resist talking about their favourite subject: themselves. Ask them, look interested and you will win a friend.

> ❝ *Few people can resist talking about their favourite*
> *subject: themselves.* ❞

Etiquette can get to be very painful if the focus is only on rules – everything from how invitations should be prepared to how to make small talk at dinner. The rules change from place to place and from time to time. The rules of etiquette are not important from a leadership perspective. The *purpose* of etiquette is important:

▶ Make the other person feel at ease.

▶ Make the other person feel valued, respected and important.

These are useful skills for a leader to have. Ultimately, good etiquette involves decentring: focus on seeing the world through the eyes of the other person. If you can do this, then you will not need rules of behaviour – you will naturally work out what is right to do in each situation.

PART TWO

The practice of leadership

4

Leading from the middle

Leaders in the middle of an organization find themselves in the dangerous world of the matrix. The brutal certainties of junior management disappear. Instead of one boss and no staff, you have two or more demanding bosses and equally demanding staff. It is no longer enough to outperform against excessive targets. In the matrix, ambiguity reigns. Nothing is what it seems. Colleagues are also your competitors for limited resources and priorities. Alliances form, shift and break in search of achieving elusive and changing goals. You have responsibility without authority or resources. You have to defy the gravity and inertia of the organization to make things happen.

If you can escape the matrix and head into the clear waters of top leadership, life becomes easier in many ways. You will have more control over your destiny. You can begin to shape the direction and goals of your organization. You can choose where to direct the resources of the organization.

&& The matrix is, arguably, the most challenging zone for a leader. The rules of success and failure change dramatically. &&

The matrix is, arguably, the most challenging zone for a leader. The rules of success and failure change dramatically. In the matrix zone of middle management, leaders are in transition. They have to move on from the rules that brought them success early in their careers. They have to prepare themselves for a new set of rules that will help them succeed at the top of the organization. In the meantime, they have to master a third set of rules that enables them to succeed in the matrix. They also have to deliver results.

The skills and behaviours of leadership are cumulative. The capabilities acquired early in the leadership journey are the foundations that support the leader in the matrix and at the top. But the early skills and behaviours need to be supplemented by more capabilities to succeed in the matrix. The leadership journey can be simplified down to three major steps:

1 *Foundations of leadership.* The challenge for the emerging leader is to learn the basics of leadership. You need to understand yourself; learn the trade of your industry; understand the culture and local rules of the game; perform against known targets.

2 *The practice of leadership.* In the middle of an organization, in the typical matrix, leaders need to learn new skills. You have to learn to manage others; manage networks, ambiguity and complexity; master core leadership skills; negotiate targets and deliver against them.

3 *Mastering leadership.* At the top of the organization, the skills of leadership change again. You have to develop an inclusive vision; be a role model for values; build the top team; create the conditions for success; acquire and direct resources to achieve the vision.

Pitfalls of survival

In the middle of the matrix the rules of success are different from the rules of survival. Many potential leaders never emerge from the matrix because they have learned how to survive within it, rather than learning how to escape from it. The five most common 'pitfalls of survival', which are also barriers to success, are listed below.

1 The expert in the matrix

Many people get promoted into the matrix on the basis of technical competency. This becomes their comfort zone. But they confuse technical expertise with management and leadership. They use their expertise to handle all the most difficult challenges in their department. A leader would figure out how to make the team rise to the challenge instead. Experts lose sight of the leadership skill of helping others achieve things, of delegation, trust and empowerment. They cannot get promoted any further because their deep technical skills are not useful in a wider context. The great IT expert can survive leading part of the IT function but is useless when faced with the challenge of managing a team of marketers, accountants and operational staff.

2 The cave dweller

Large organizations often have silos which divide groups vertically, by region, product or function. They are also layered like pancakes: the flat organization is an illusion of being in a pancake. Many 'flat' organizations are towering layers of pancakes. Corporately, if you cross a silo with a pancake, you get a cave. This is where some people decide to hide: they can survive the matrix, but they cannot escape from it. They can control and dominate their little cave and recreate the certainty that served them so well at junior management levels. These territorial types guard their caves jealously. When the reorganization comes along and the matrix changes shape, they are like fish out of water. They are very easy to rationalize out of the organization.

3 The politician

Politicians are too enthusiastic about learning the dark arts of the matrix. They work assiduously to cultivate a power network. They constantly look out for new initiatives: they make sure they are associated closely enough with all of them to share some of the limelight if it works, but far enough away that they share none of the blame if it goes wrong. Being associated with success and achieving success are different. Ultimately, many politicians are undone because they are seen to be like a can with a pea in it: they are empty vessels making a lot of noise. They achieve nothing. Worse, the politicking eventually backfires; it gains enemies who are only too happy to come out of the woodwork at the worst possible time for the politician.

4 The boy scout

The boy scout is the opposite of the politician. The boy scout thinks that by working hard and delivering results they will automatically be recognized and promoted. In practice, they simply get lost in the matrix, where it is often difficult to see who has really achieved what. They are naïve. They need a claim to fame, but they also need to stake their claim; they need to show that they are really leading and delivering.

5 The autocrat

The autocrat acts is if they are already a senior leader. They often talk about the importance of being a team player. By this they mean: 'If you do exactly what I tell you to, you are a good team player. If you show less than 100% personal loyalty to me, you are not a team player.' For these people, performance is essential. If they deliver exceptional results, they may well progress. If they deliver less than excellent results, they will just be seen as a dysfunctional pain in the backside by those above, below and beside them.

The path through the matrix

One way or the other, there are many roads to ruin within the matrix. Picking the right path for the leadership journey through the matrix is seriously difficult. At the risk of stretching the bounds of intellectual integrity, we will return to the three and a half Ps framework to find the path through the matrix.

The success route through the matrix looks like this:

Focusing on people

Matrix leaders learn how to achieve results through other people. They may have formal authority over some people. More important, leaders achieve results through people over whom they have no formal authority. They learn the subtle arts of motivating and coaching people they are responsible for, and they learn the art of networking and influencing people over whom they have no formal control.

Being professional

Matrix leaders start to model the values that they will need as senior leaders. They also master some core skills of management and leadership, which are as simple as running: reading, writing, talking and listening skills. Most of us can run; few can win an Olympic gold for running. The leader can do at least some of the basics, like chairing meetings, very well.

Being positive

In the middle of the matrix, the art of being positive is particularly important. Here, it means treating ambiguity and change as an opportunity, not a risk. Matrix leaders learn how to deal with conflict, which is endemic in the matrix, and how to deal with crises, which are inevitable. The positive outlook of the successful matrix leader is what distinguishes them from the survivalist matrix manager. The survivalist will avoid risk and ambiguity. The successful leader will take on risk, change and ambiguity. The survivalist is on the slow road to nowhere. Leaders enjoy significant career acceleration: they succeed fast or they fail fast.

❝ *The successful leader will take on risk,*
change and ambiguity. **❞**

Finally, we dare not forget the half *P*: performance. To emerge from the matrix, you need a claim to fame. You need to show that you can deliver exceptional results out of exceptional ambiguity and complexity. It is only through taking on challenges and delivering results that you can learn the subtle arts of people focus, being positive and professionalism. Achieving results and achieving learning go hand in hand.

In the next three chapters, we will plot a path through the matrix using the three and a half *P*s as a map. Here, more than ever, a guide is essential.

5

Focusing on people

Churchill described Russia as a 'riddle, wrapped in a mystery, inside an enigma'. He may as well have been describing human nature. The collective efforts of tens of thousands of shrinks over the last hundred years have not made people happier or more motivated. They have shown that we are all more messed up than we ever thought. Stress, low self-esteem, depression and other mental dysfunctions are at epidemic levels.

All the leader must do is to solve the riddle wrapped in the mystery inside the enigma. The leader has to succeed where all the shrinks have failed; your riddle is to find a way of motivating all your people.

To solve this we will look at three approaches:

1 Three practical theories of motivation.
2 How leaders apply the theory in practice.
3 Motivation and moments of truth.

Before we embark on the journey in search of motivation, it is worth being clear about what motivation is and is not. It helps if we are searching for the right thing.

Motivation is not inspiration. There is too much talk about inspirational leaders. There *are* some inspirational leaders out there, but most of us are not natural inspirers. We can do many basic things well which will motivate people. We may even inspire people if we do the basics well enough. But if we set off in search of inspiration we are likely to find ourselves in the land of men in white suits waving their arms on stages, whipping massed audiences into a frenzy of excitement. They can sell inspiration, insurance or religion with equal vigour. Sustaining motivation for the weeks, months and years that follow the speech is a different art form.

Motivation is also not about influencing skills, which we have already discovered. Influencing skills are largely transactional. They are a one-off event aimed at getting agreement to a specific task or idea. Motivation is much more about building a sustained relationship. You want motivated people to do the right thing consistently without always having to cajole and persuade them. Motivation takes more time and investment but pays higher dividends in the long run.

Practical theories of motivation: part one

Let's start with a simple choice.

Let us assume that you are a budding leader who likes work, is committed to it, lives to work and to lead and is deeply involved in your business. Look around you. Not just at your peers, but also look at people at all levels of your organization. If they are all like you in their attitude to your organization, pick Y.

If you think people fundamentally dislike work, are lazy, work to live and feel alienated from work, pick X.

Obviously, how you motivate people will depend on whether you think they are X-types or Y-types. It is possible you are surrounded by a mixture of the two.

Let's start with the X-types. In a perfect world, you would be able to convert them into happy, zealous Y-types. We may land up in a perfect world when we die. In the meantime, we have to deal with the X-types. The traditional response to the X-types is to have tight control, close monitoring, minimal delegation and clear rewards and punishments for success and failure. There are still plenty of bosses who will assume that everyone who works for them is an X-type. They are highly controlling and demanding. They may not be fun to work for, but they can work their way up the career ladder.

Y-types can be managed differently. They can be trusted to do their best as committed colleagues. Trust, empowerment and delegation take the place of control.

This exploration of the X and Y worlds is based on McGregor's *Human Side of Enterprise* (1960), which remains a classic description of different types of motivation at work. Increasingly, much of the world is moving from X to Y. The cynical, untrusting world of the X-type is perhaps typical of the nineteenth-century sweatshop where uneducated masses were hired for their hands, not their brains. The bosses bossed and the workers worked. In some cases the workers revolted and got exploited by tyrannical governments instead of tyrannical capitalists. In the West, the workers got educated. So now we see more of theory Y world, where workers work in offices and with their brains. We need more than compliance – we need commitment. We need their talent to work through the increasing complexity and confusion of modern work.

McGregor focused on the worker. But what works for the worker should also work for the leader. Although the world may be moving from X to Y, many managers feel much more comfortable in X mode. Look at the two types of management below and decide which you are. Also, decide which type of boss you would prefer to work for.

Management criteria	X-type manager	Y-type leader
Basis of power	Formal authority	Authority and respect
Focus of control	Process compliance	Outcomes, achievement
Communication style	One-way: tell and do	Two-way: tell and listen
Success criteria	Make no mistakes	Beat targets
Attention to detail	High	Moderate
Ambiguity tolerance	Minimal	Moderate
Political ability	Moderate	High
Preferred structure	Hierarchy	Network

Figure 5.1 Types of management

Many people instinctively prefer the more inspirational Y-type leader. I have worked for both. The Y-type leader was much more demanding. They may forgive the occasional mistake, but overall their expectations are much higher. The X-type was a mean and nasty apology of a manager. But working for him was a simple matter of keeping your nose clean, doing what you were told and no more, and being blindly loyal and obedient. He expected compliance, not commitment. The Y-type expected commitment and would tolerate occasional non-compliance if that helped achieve a goal.

The catch is that both types of leader can succeed, in the right context. The X-type manager succeeds in a classic machine bureaucracy where the emphasis is on avoiding mistakes and achieving predictability and control. Systems integration houses, insurance companies and large parts of the public sector fit this style.

The Y-type leader fits where there is a need to change and to adapt to different and uncertain customer and competitive pressures. This better describes creative agencies, entrepreneurial organizations and professional service firms. The Y-type leader explodes in the X-type environment and vice versa. You have to find the environment where your style will work.

Practical theories of motivation: part two

McGregor's X- and Y-types find an echo in Herzberg's two-factor theory of motivation. As a leader, he argued, you can motivate people in one of two ways. Pick which you think works in your organization:

Option One

Make sure individuals have the status and title and terms and conditions which they deserve. Pay for performance, and pay a bonus for over-performance. Use hours, holidays, flexitime and family-friendly work policies to get the right balance of staff. This is classic rational management. It is the sort of thing that public sector unions like to discuss with public sector employers.

The problem with Option One is that this is a never-ending treadmill. Once someone has got the pay rise and the bonus, then they want the shorter working hours. Herzberg called these 'hygiene factors'. In practice, not only do they do little to motivate but they can be demotivators. Bad pay and conditions demotivate; good pay and conditions are never sufficient to produce stellar performance.

Despite this, many organizations still use pay and bonuses as a substitute for management or motivation. Pay discussions sound very managerial: senior executives sit round a table discussing people (like managers should) and performance (like managers should) and make decisions (like managers should) about money (very managerial). And at the end of several hours in a sweaty room and locked in mortal combat over the bonus scheme, they successfully irritate everyone. Pay a successful trader or fund manager a £100,000 bonus and they may promptly resign (after the money is in their bank account) when they find that one of their peers has got a £120,000 bonus. Money ceases to be a necessity: it becomes a way of measuring the worth of an individual. No one likes being told that they are worth less than someone else, especially if they have the city-sized ego of a trader or fund manager.

❝ No one likes being told that they are worth less than someone else. ❞

Option Two

Focus on the intrinsic rewards, recognition and value of the job, creating a sense of community and belonging. This can achieve exceptional results at exceptionally low cost. Many vocational careers, like the army, teaching and academia, pay poorly but can attract exceptional talent and achieve exceptional results. Some of the best and brightest graduates go off to work as underpaid researchers for politicians or work for peanuts in the glamorous world of the international auction houses.

The choice between these two options goes to the heart of current discussions about stress, employee protection and regulation. The received wisdom is that employees need to be protected by regulation from the harsh winds of the marketplace. Flexi time, family-friendly policies and shorter working weeks are all part of this trend. There are few people who would want to reverse this. The public sector sets the best practice example in terms of working hours, flexi time and being family friendly. It is also suffers by far the highest rates of absenteeism, sickness and stress-related complaints. Focusing on Option One may be important, but in the case of the public sector, it is clearly not enough to motivate staff.

Conversely, it is clear that many people are quite happy to seek out what appear to be stressful careers. The modern professions, from accounting through law, consulting and finance all put new graduates through sweat-it-out apprenticeships. And they are overwhelmed with demand for positions. These are classic Option Two-type careers: the hours may be antisocial and the demands may be extreme, but the opportunities are great. If people see that they are doing something worthwhile in an organization that has prospects and they have some control over their future, that goes a long way to making up for the lack of an on-site crèche. Conversely, put someone in an organization under siege (much of the public sector), with limited career prospects and limited autonomy, and the only sources of motivation are essentially Option One-type bribes: more money, easier conditions. This is fertile ground for strikes and conflict.

For the leader, this contrast between Option One and Option Two is critical. The easy way out for all leaders is to go down Option One routes: more money, easy terms. The motivation lasts as long as it takes for the bonus to hit the bank account. The harder route, but which sustains motivation longer, is Option Two: give people meaningful work, create a sense of belonging, opportunity and recognition and you are more likely to motivate. The cynics will argue that you will be able to exploit people better – more work for modest pay.

As a leader in the middle of the organization, there is not much you can do to change Option One. You have to make the most of the hand you have been dealt by the organization. You have to deploy some of the motivational skills in Option Two.

Case*Study* Teach First: making a motivational offering

At first sight, Teach First had perhaps the least attractive recruiting proposition ever devised for top graduates. It asked them to do two years teaching in the most challenging schools in London with some of the most disadvantaged children. They received six weeks training, which meant giving up any chance of holiday after graduation. Most teacher training programmes take two years. They would be paid about half what they would receive if they joined a top-flight consulting firm. Teach First lacked the prestige of the big recruiters. It was a start up – no one had heard of it. It was a charity. It had a tiny budget.

In its first year, over 5% of Oxbridge and Imperial final-year undergraduates with good degrees had applied. At the time, no graduates from these universities were teaching in the target schools. In its second year, it was the youngest organization and only charity in *The Times* ranking of the top 50 graduate recruiters. The next youngest top recruiter was Microsoft. Dropout rates were low and enthusiasm of the new teachers was high, despite the huge stress and challenges they faced on a daily basis.

Why should high flying graduates be motivated to join such an unlikely scheme, against better paid offerings, and why did they feel motivated to stay in the scheme even after the reality of working in the challenging schools became clear?

The good news is that there are graduates out there who have a conscience and have good social values. Teach First gave them a chance to make a worthwhile contribution. But that was never going to be enough. They may have hearts, but they also have heads. Teach First is designed to develop graduates into leaders of the future. It gives them far more practical experience of core leadership skills such as motivating, influencing, dealing with conflict and surviving adversity than any amount of staring into computer screens will do. Trading bonds or writing reports may make money, but at the end of two years it will be the Teach First participants who are prepared for leadership, not the highly paid galley slaves chained to their computers.

To make this promise credible, many top recruiters in consulting, investment banking and law supported Teach First. The participants are also heavily supported with teaching mentors, business internship, a one week micro-MBA and leadership training. This takes up more of their limited free time. So the participants do not get huge pay and they do not get huge holidays. They do very poorly on Herzberg's Option One route: good money and easy hours. They do very well on Option Two: they have a meaningful job, they have real prospects, they are highly recognized and they are given high autonomy and responsibility. Option Two is very hard work for the employer and the employed. It can have dramatic results.

Practical theories of motivation: part three

Life is a little more subtle than flipping a coin and choosing between X and Y. Different people have different needs at different times.

I learned about how needs differ at an early stage. I set out for India in search of enlightenment. I got to Afghanistan and ran out of money. This was in the days before there were mobile phones for the emotionally incontinent and credit cards for the financially feckless. My interest in enlightenment plummeted and my interest in money soared. So I sold my blood, but not my soul, to the locals. I got money, not enlightenment, and was grateful for it.

For the rich and successful, survival is taken for granted. Many seek immortality by buying up art collections, endowing charities and naming universities, buildings and departments after themselves. Most of us are in between those two extremes most of the time. We want to be paid, we want to feel a sense of belonging to something worthwhile and we would like to be recognized for what we do.

Perhaps all this is obvious. So it is refreshing to find that this is a case of practical theory from Maslow's hierarchy of needs.

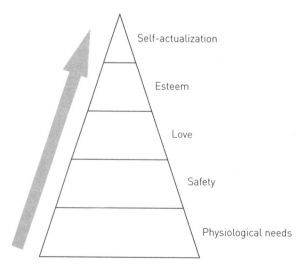

Figure 5.2 Maslow's hierarchy of needs

Maslow argued that we are all needs junkies. We want to climb the ladder of needs from survival to immortality. Let us climb the ladder with him, converting his language into the language of leaders.

▶ *Physiological needs* for Maslow are items like food and water: without them we get hungry and thirsty. Pay and conditions are the food and water of the employment world.

▶ *Safety* is a sense of security which comes in part from the employer and also from knowing that you have the skills to do the job. If the worst comes to the worst, they are skills which you can use elsewhere.

▶ *Love* can be dangerous at work. So instead of loving your staff, it is enough to make sure that they have a sense of belonging and community. They are trusted and respected for who they are. At its most basic, this is about leaders taking a positive interest in the careers and lives of those they are responsible for.

▶ *Esteem* is about recognizing and rewarding individuals. The old saying holds true: 'Praise in public, criticise in private.' One leader makes sure that he praises ten times as often as he criticizes. Sometimes he finds it difficult. But once you start looking, there is usually much to praise and be thankful for.

▶ *Self-actualization* is about achievement – creating a legacy which is meaningful and recognized.

> **❝ One leader makes sure that he praises ten times as often as he criticizes. ❞**

If you asked a leader what each rung of Maslow's hierarchy of needs was about, they would not know. But effective leaders understand this model intuitively, and they play to it.

Overleaf is an unauthorized version of the model converted into the reality of the work place.

Everyone has something more they want. Everyone has something they fear. We fear a project going wrong, or a supplier or staff member failing us. We fear losing our jobs sometimes. We fear being left behind in the leadership marathon by our peers. There is always something we fear.

Figure 5.3 Maslow's hierarchy of needs (the unauthorized, revisionist, leadership version)

There is also always something we want. Perhaps many of us would really like to become billionaires, Oscar winners, sports stars or astronauts. All at the same time. But these things are not easy. We are always making a trade-off between what we want and the risk and effort involved in getting there. We are risk averse (we fear failure) and we prefer things to be made easier, not more difficult.

Some leaders use the fear part of the equation most. Fear-based leaders stress the negative: 'If you don't…' or 'You can't afford to get this wrong…'. In the short term, this can be highly effective. Eventually, however, people burn out, stress out and walk out. Meanwhile, the fear-based leader has achieved results and may well have moved onwards and upwards to greater things. They climb to the top over the career corpses of those they have killed.

Other leaders use the greed element most. Greed is not just about money: it is about ego, recognition and immortality. Having a professorial chair or a museum named after you is greed fulfilled, for a while. Even at the top of a career, there is hunger for something more: most CEOs are not content to be mere custodians of a legacy they have inherited. They want to create their own legacy. They crave more recognition. This way, disaster can lie. The lure of greatness is a distraction from the obligation to deliver.

Finally, good leaders use idleness to their advantage in two ways.

First, good leaders do not make life difficult for their followers. They are clear about what they want, where they are going and how to get there. They give structure and guidance to their teams to minimize wasted effort. They help clear the way forward with the rest of the organization by removing political obstacles and aligning other parts of the organization with what they are trying to achieve. They set their followers up for success.

Second, good leaders do not interfere with their teams. They do not over-manage. They give teams discretion within a structure. The leader risks looking idle, because they let go. This is a very hard lesson for many leaders to learn. The classic trap is that of the 'leader in the locker room'. The leader in the locker room is like the footballer that becomes the team manager. In his head, he is still one of the players. He does not want to give up the familiar world of the locker room. But he has to learn that as manager he has other things to do: he has to focus on training, coaching, hiring, firing, team selection, competitor analysis. The technical skills that made him a great player are not the same skills he needs to become a great manager.

One popular form of good leadership is 'MBWA', or Management By Walking Around. MBWA can create the leader-in-the-locker-room problem. Arguably, the opposite of MBWA is required: Management By Walking Away. For a leader, this is nerve-racking; you direct a team to do something, and you want to see how it is doing. You want to pull the seed up every few moments to see how it is progressing. Leave it alone. Be available for help, but do not interfere. The end result may not be exactly what you predicted; it may be better. By not interfering, you show you trust the team, they feel motivated, they do their best and they learn more by trying to do things themselves than by blindly following your exact orders.

Maslow can be complicated. In practice leaders cannot go round calculating if each person is at the love stage or the self-actualization stage, let alone know what to do about it. Going into a board room and asking which board members are at the love level would be original, if not totally advisable or actionable. The simpler way is to remember three things: fear, greed and idleness.

Work on people's hopes. Work on people's fears – humane leaders seek to remove risk and remove fear. Inhumane leaders happily stoke up fear. Finally, put idleness to work. Make things easy for others: give a clear structure and direction. Make it easy for yourself: do not over-manage. Fear, greed and idleness work as much for selling ideas as they do for motivating people. If your idea appeals to someone's hopes, removes a fear and you make it easy for them to say 'yes', they are likely to say 'yes'.

Leaders may not understand or care for the theory. They just put it into practice.

How leaders apply the theory in practice

We have looked at what the theory of leadership says. Now let's hear what leaders say about human nature.

First, in our survey of over 700 current and emerging leaders, the most important quality valued in a leader was the ability to motivate others. When we asked our participants how satisfied they were with the motivational capabilities of their leaders, we found a huge motivation gap. Although motivation was seen as the most important attribute of a leader, only 37% were satisfied with the performance of their leaders in this respect. Clearly, there was a problem.

We looked further to find out more about what people expected in terms of motivation, and then we looked at specific situations to see how well or poorly they were handled.

We asked people about leaders who had motivated them and leaders who had not motivated them. This is what they expected:

1 My boss shows an interest in my career.

2 I trust my boss: (s)he is honest with me.

3 I know where we are going and how to get there.

4 I am doing a worthwhile job.

5 I am recognized for my contribution.

We will look at each briefly. But first let's look at what is not there:

▶ Money: when it was mentioned, it was seen as a de-motivator, not a motivator. Get the money wrong and you send a signal that either you cannot be trusted to deliver on a promise or that you do not value the person highly enough relative to their peers. Either way, you have broken trust, and your credibility as a leader of that person is lost.

▶ Family-friendly hours, shorter hours, flexi time, facilities: these simply did not appear on the radar screen. People who have signed up for the leadership journey have signed up for some self-sacrifice and are also good at compartmentalizing their lives. They do not share personal concerns in a professional environment. If they have doubts, they conceal them until they have decided to leave.

Look again at the list of expectations that followers have of leaders when it comes to motivation. It is very simple. There are no dark arts to be learned in leading people. Treat them and care for them as humans, and the chances are that they will respond. We will look at each expectation in turn:

My boss shows an interest in my career

Hierarchical relationships are unequal. You are more important to your followers than they are to you. Their jobs and livelihoods depend on you: the reverse is only partially and indirectly true. It also means that you probably focus intently on managing your boss, but less intently on managing downwards. Most people know more about their bosses than they do about their followers.

As a follower, if your boss is clearly not interested in your career, it is unnerving.

Normally, there is an implicit psychological contract between leader and follower, which is far more important than any job description. The contract says that the follower will do what it takes to support the leader, and the leader will look after the pay, promotion and assignment prospects of the follower. If the leader is either unwilling or unable to deliver on the leader's half of the contract, there is little incentive for the follower to feel good about following.

Some leaders make this contract highly explicit. In return they demand absolute loyalty. They create a personal fiefdom. At promotion and bonus councils they will play very hard to deliver the promises they made to their teams. The result can be somewhat dysfunctional: a power baron with his own team emerges, playing to his own rules, with his own team. The team will tend to show great loyalty to a leader who looks after them so well. The team becomes a cult: inward looking, demanding, and divisive with the rest of the organization.

I trust my boss: (s)he is honest with me

Honesty and *business* are not words that are often heard together in the media. But all the leaders I interviewed, even in industries such as investment banking, stressed honesty. This is not about honour and ethics and being nice to the planet. This is much more hard-faced and practical.

Followers want to know where they stand. If they have been working hard for a year and think they are doing fine, it is devastating if the boss turns up at the annual review and gives an unsatisfactory ranking. The boss has been dishonest. Dishonesty is not about lying; it is about failing to tell the whole truth, even the uncomfortable truth, promptly. This is an honesty test that would cause panic for some politicians.

> **"** *Dishonesty is not about lying; it is about failing to tell the whole truth, even the uncomfortable truth, promptly.* **"**

Honesty is ultimately about trust. If you do not trust someone, it becomes very hard to work for them as a leader.

I know where we are going and how to get there

Sometimes this is called 'vision'. But vision is too grand: it sounds like Moses, Martin Luther King and Gandhi all rolled together. Provide a simple description of where your team has to get to on the next three-month project. Let your people know what they need to develop personally over the next six months and the practical actions they can take to develop those skills. Show where your business is going over the next one to three years. Do these things and you start to give people the clarity, structure and direction they need. Put it the other way: if your people do not know where they are going or how they are going to get there, they are soon going to become very frustrated.

I am doing a worthwhile job

Not everyone gets to do exciting, high-powered jobs all the time. Some jobs are plain dull, tedious, stressful or unglamorous. But they need to be done.

The world of repairing shoes is perhaps not the most exciting. Go to a shoe repair shop, and the conditions are hardly brilliant. Some of them are little more than holes in the wall. Staff tend to be on wages which are modest by any standards, and would be small change for a banker. And yet Timpson manages to create a loyal workforce in his shoe repair shops and he is widely regarded as a very good leader. One of the many things he does is to focus on customer satisfaction and constantly recognize and reward great service: he always has a supply of prizes available in his car. His staff focus on the positive impact they are having on customers; each happy customer is evidence that they are doing a worthwhile job.

In investment banking there are plenty of dull jobs to be done in checking documents: the dullness is offset by knowing that a billion-dollar deal may fail if you get it wrong. Even dull stuff can be made worthwhile in the right context.

I am recognized for my contribution

Let's make this simple. If you never get any recognition for all your efforts, you get upset. You probably do not feel very motivated to put in more effort. So recognize the efforts of your team. Some leaders feel the need to grab all the glory if their teams do well: they are also the leaders who are the first to walk away and delegate blame if things go wrong. Strong leaders have the self-confidence to recognize the success of their teams. Recognizing success is effective because:

▶ it shows the leader has built a strong and effective team

▶ it motivates the team.

Recognition takes multiple forms: it can be as simple as a few well chosen words in front of the CEO. Take time to say thank you, and to mean it, to the individual or team directly. Recognition can also be prizes, newsletter mentions or celebrations at a night out. Pay rises are often the least effective form of recognition because in most organizations they are not public knowledge.

Motivation and moments of truth

In any relationship there are moments of truth. This is when you discover the real nature of the other person. The moment of truth can come at any time. Both our leaders and followers identified three classic moments of truth in the leader–follower relationship:

1 Payback time

2 Feedback time: formal and informal

3 Problem time: the screaming monkeys

Payback time

As a leader you are making an implicit, sometimes explicit, promise to look after the interests of your followers. Fail to deliver for them, and you are a failure, not a leader, to them.

We have already seen how some leaders play hard ball for their followers at promotion and bonus time. One budding power baron played this game to perfection. Essentially, he rigged the process. He worked out all the evaluation criteria and wrote evaluations which were designed to score maximum points for his followers. Anyone who had been disloyal got lousy evaluations, even if they were very good. He then backed his evaluations all the way. It was impossible to argue with him; his followers had only worked for him so there was no other point of view. The only benchmarks were the lousy reviews he had written for disloyal people who had gone on to succeed elsewhere: this was evidence, he claimed, that his evaluation criteria were tougher than anyone else's. He delivered results to his teams, who wisely remained loyal to him.

Other promises are just as important. Once, I found myself earning real sweat equity in Riyadh, Saudi Arabia. The project went well. The client wanted to go to a second stage. The partner came in at the end of the first project expecting to agree the second stage with the client. I dreaded the meeting: I had planned a great holiday as an escape from all the hard work. The partner knew this, but I could see economic necessity would outweigh personal need. The moment of truth came. The client agreed to the second stage, and my heart sank.

Then the partner turned to the client and said, 'Of course, you don't mind starting phase two later so that Jo can have his holiday, do you?'

The client was delighted: suddenly he saw me as a human (you can fool some of the people...) not just a work drudge. My relationship with the client improved further. More important, I realized I had discovered a partner I could trust. We worked together on and off for the next ten years.

*&& Always deliver on expectations. **

Always deliver on expectations. We do it for our bosses, even if the expectation is unwritten and scarcely hoped for by the boss. We should do the same for our followers if we want to earn their loyalty.

Feedback time

Formal feedback

Giving positive feedback is easy. People like receiving it. People like giving it. The test of the leader is not praising followers, rather it is helping them through some of their professional challenges. Giving negative feedback is deeply uncomfortable for most people; there are few leaders who seem to relish such opportunities. We are not even meant to talk about negative feedback. We retreat into the comfort of obscurity and jargon. We talk about development opportunities. If someone has really messed up, we might talk about development challenges. When we are close to firing them, we concede they have performance challenges.

Most feedback and most assessments are fundamentally dishonest. In one consulting firm 95% of staff are routinely rated as 'above average' or better. This is mathematically impossible, but politically inevitable. No one thinks of themselves as average. Do a quick test. Think of your peer group. Compared to them, do you really think that you are a below-average worker, lover, driver, thinker or human being? How many of your peers will think they are below average?

Most people land up being dishonest in giving reviews. It is emotionally necessary for the reviewee and the reviewer, and it is politically necessary given the way the system works if you are to fulfil your pay and promotion promises to your staff. Administratively it is necessary, because nearly all assessment systems are run like school reports – they grade people on some sort of good/bad continuum.

In practice, we have found only one effective alternative to the school report system – use a development grid. At each level of an organization people develop, going through stages like this:

- ▶ new
- ▶ developing
- ▶ maturing
- ▶ mature.

This development happens across the whole range of skills and competencies required in the role, such as problem solving, team work and team management. If you rank someone who has been one year in the role as a mixture of 'new' or 'developing' there is likely to be little argument. There will be constructive discussion about how to progress on all the development criteria. On a traditional assessment, if you ranked the same person as 1 or 2 out of a 4-point scale on the same criteria, it would be toys out of pram time. The arguing, shouting and demands for an appeal and impartial assessment would be deafening. Of course, the two assessments are essentially the same. However, the development assessment is positive and constructive while the traditional assessment is negative and confrontational. In an organization which is stuck with the traditional system, it is possible to run an informal development system alongside the formal system. Just be sure not to tell HR what you are doing.

The development assessment is more challenging to staff than the traditional system. But it provides a non-confrontational way of giving constructive criticism to them. It helps you to be honest with them. If you are honest, you will build trust. Staff will be in danger of thinking that you are a good leader.

Informal feedback

If a formal assessment is a surprise, it is a failure. By the time someone arrives at the formal review, they should be roughly aware of where they stand. If they do not know where they stand, then the formal review is likely to degenerate into argument rather than constructive discussion about the way forward. They are likely to lose trust in you; they will feel that you have not been honest with them during the review period in highlighting concerns and issues as they arose.

The art of informal feedback is essential for a leader. Regular feedback sets expectations and helps the individual keep on the performance track. But once again we are left with the problem that giving and receiving negative feedback is unpleasant. So we avoid it. The closest some leaders get to giving negative feedback is by showing frustration or anger when things go wrong. This helps no one, as no one knows what to do differently besides working harder and not upsetting the boss. So how can you do it? Negative feedback can cover anything from being irritated that a colleague slurps soup at his desk during lunch to helping someone see that the presentation they think is brilliant might need to be rewritten.

In moments of stress – and negative feedback is stressful – it helps to have a system to fall back on. You can create your own version of it. I tend to use a simple acronym for mine: SPIN.

> **S**ituation specifics
>
> **P**ersonal impact
>
> **I**nsight and interpretation
>
> **N**ext steps.

Situation

First, make sure the situation is right. If the other person is shouting and screaming, it is not a good time to throw fuel on the fire with a little negative feedback. Talk when the other person is calm. But try to do so as close to the event as possible. Feedback, like milk, goes off fairly quickly.

Second, be specific about exactly what happened. Telling someone they are 'unprofessional' is unhelpful and provocative. If you note that they have turned up more than ten minutes late for the last five meetings, you have something specific to talk about.

Personal impact

Having established that the person is habitually late, it is tempting to say that they are unprofessional. This leads straight back to the shouting match. Instead, focus on how it makes you feel: you can argue with judgements, not with feelings. If you say, 'It makes me feel that you do not think client or management meetings are important', the worst you risk is a 'So what?' in return. You can follow up and ask if that is the impression they meant to create. If there is still no appropriate reaction, stop. Try again at a time and a place where they will be more responsive.

Insight and interpretation

It is now tempting to tell people what to do: don't. Instead, ask the individual if that is the impact they intend to make or whether they want to make another impact. Do not tell them what to do; let them figure it out. They will value their solutions much more than they value your solutions. If they want your help, they will ask for it.

Next steps

By this point, you should be ready for a relatively calm way of agreeing next steps. Land up on a future-focused, positive and constructive agenda, rather than a backwards-looking blame game.

Take time in applying this model. Do not move from one step to the next until the other person is ready to move on. If the situation is wrong and they disagree with the basic facts, then find a better time and go back and confirm the facts. It is possible that they are right and you are wrong.

Problem time: the screaming monkeys

This is the final test of the leader, and it is very easy to fail. It happens when staff come to you with a problem. Like any good leader, you make sure that you are available for advice. So you are pleased to see someone come through your open door with a problem. You are even more pleased when they walk back out of the door again with the problem lifted from their shoulders. Congratulations. You have just failed the test. Failed? When I did everything right? Are you nuts?

Let's call up the slow motion replay and see why the referee awarded the penalty against you.

A member of staff comes into your office. She has a monkey on her back. It is a screaming monkey and behaving badly. She needs help. So you take the monkey off her back. You now have the monkey and she leaves happy. Hearing that you are in a good mood, another staffer comes in. He has two screaming monkeys: one on each shoulder. You lift the burden from his shoulders. You now have three screaming monkeys in your office. By the end of the day, you have a vast troupe of monkeys in your office. Your staff are very happy, and you are very unhappy.

The leader is not there to solve every problem. You have assembled a team to solve the problems for you. You may have the most expertise, but avoid the temptation to become the leader in the locker room. You need to raise your game and focus on the wider issues facing the team – making sure they are working on the right problem, making sure you have the right team, making sure they have the right support and development. Only if you force them to solve the problem themselves will they develop the skills and confidence to become effective.

« Only if you force them to solve the problem themselves will they develop the skills and confidence to become effective. »

When the staff person comes into the office with a monkey, give them advice and coaching on how to deal with the monkey. This is neither quick nor easy. It will take careful questioning to understand their problem and to help them understand it properly as well. It is probably easier in the short term to deal with the problem yourself: to take the monkey off their backs. But make sure they deal with the monkey themselves. If you are really smart, invite them to take with them one of the monkeys you have. It could be a good development opportunity for them. By the end of the day, you will have succeeded if there are no more screaming monkeys in your room.

The essence of this approach is to coach people through their problems, not to solve their problems even if you think you know the answer. If you solve all their problems for them, they never learn or develop as individuals. Neither will they have any ownership over your solution; they will lack commitment and belief. Coaching them through their problem helps them learn and develop and it ensures that they have ownership of whatever solution they eventually discover. As they become more adept at solving problems themselves, so they will rely less on coming to you for help. In the short term coaching is high effort, but it pays big long-term dividends.

6

Being positive

Leading in the middle of an organization can be gruelling. It is like the middle of a chess game. The start is clear, and there are well-known openings which you can pick. As a pawn, you advance steadily up the board. If you have picked the wrong opening or are in the wrong place at the wrong time, you get taken out. You have to start a new game. The end game is also clearer. Hopefully, you will be the king or queen of the board. Success or failure revolves entirely around you and you can control your destiny.

In the middle, you are like a knight going out to do battle for your organization. But everything is complicated. The board is crowded with other players. You are meant to achieve much with little power. Your career is a zigzag. You no longer advance in a straight line. Like the chess knight, sometimes you take two steps to the side and one forward. Sometimes you even take one step back and two to the side to get round a blockage and find another opportunity to advance.

The knight's life is one of crises, conflicts, risks and ambiguity. And the knight is meant to perform, have influence and use power. Delivering against this requires a combination of positive behaviours and skills, which are the focus of this chapter. We will explore four major themes:

1 Handling conflicts, crises and risks.

2 Managing projects.

3 Managing change.

4 Building power, influence and networks.

These are all core skills that leaders need to acquire. The battle-hardened veteran leader will tell you that the only way to build these skills is through experience. The veteran will be right. But it makes sense to prepare for the inevitable crises and conflicts. Going into treacherous waters without a map is a recipe for career shipwreck.

Handling conflicts, crises and risks

Conflicts

There are conflicts in the best-run organizations. The leader should be highly suspicious if there is no conflict, because organizations are set up for conflict.

Let's emphasize the point: organizations are set up for conflict.

In any organization there is a limited pot of money, management time, skills and resources. Different products, functions and regions will inevitably have different perspectives and priorities. They are all bidding for the same limited resource pot. The ensuing bidding war between departments may be civilized or it may be underhand, political and nasty. In any event, there is a contest and a conflict going on. For many leaders in the middle, the competition is not some abstract organization in the market place. The real competition is sitting at a desk nearby, competing for the same resources and the same promotion. That is much more serious competition for the leader.

If we recognize that conflict is a natural fact of life in any organization, we can take the first step towards dealing with it. Conflict is not about people or personalities: it is about positions and priorities.

I asked all our leaders how they dealt with conflict. They all homed in on the same set of principles:

❝Never avoid conflict. Embrace it. It develops the leadership and interpersonal skills of the emerging leader.❞

▶ Never avoid conflict. Embrace it. Conflict is how priorities are set and decisions are made. It develops the leadership and interpersonal skills of the emerging leader.

▶ Depersonalize the conflict. Never take conflict personally, even if it is meant that way. Focus on the issues and interests at stake, not the personalities.

▶ Detach yourself. Observe what is happening and do not get emotionally involved. Lose your temper, lose the argument. Think how a leader or role model you admire would handle the situation. One leader called this 'putting on the mask of leadership'. You may have boiling emotions inside, but present the mask of your ideal leader and use that to guide your actions.

Occasionally, some conflicts do get emotional and unpleasant. Humans, unlike computers, do have emotions. These events are rare but dangerous. If they are mishandled, even the innocent party gets tainted by the event. At times like this, a simple model helps as a guide. Try to remember this:

FEAR TO EAR

FEAR stands for the natural reaction to outright hostility. It also stands for how we feel before seeing the CEO for the first time. It is a helpful emotion when our ancestors faced a sabre tooth tiger; it would alert them to fight or flight. Fighting or fleeing at the first sight of the CEO is not helpful.

The wrong response is to let FEAR take over, as follows:

Fight furiously.

Engage enemy emotionally.

Argue against anyone.

Retaliate, refute, repudiate reason

If it is your last day at work, the preceding is a good way to go down. However, take the F out of FEAR and you are left with EAR, which is what you should use to start listening. EAR stands for:

Empathize

Agree the problem

Resolve the way forward

The temptation is to go straight to resolving the way forward. This simply invites more argument; the other side will knock down anything you say. You need to calm them down. Empathize with them. This does not mean hugging them. It means using active listening skills, which will be covered in the next chapter. As you listen, you will find out more about the real nature of their difficulty and why they feel so threatened. Do not try to argue: try to understand. Win a friend, not an argument. Once you have won a friend, you have a chance of winning the argument if there is any substantive argument beneath the emotional froth. You cannot begin to find a solution until you have found the problem which you both can agree on. Once you have agreed the root cause of the problem together, you have a chance of finding a way forward.

Crises

Some people are lucky; they never encounter a real career or business crisis. Most people find that they do have a crisis at some point in their careers. It can feel very lonely. The only person who can get you out of the crisis is yourself. The middle of the organization is where many emerging leaders find themselves bailing out to set up their organic pig farm in North Wales. This is natural. The first flush of career enthusiasm has disappeared. The long haul to the top still looks long. Then something happens: the final straw is added to the camel's back.

The difference between success and failure sometimes comes down to persistence. Successful leaders work through their crises and find that Nietzsche was right: 'That which does not break you, makes you stronger.' Others are mucking out the organic waste on their pig farms.

The best way to prepare for crises is to develop resilience early. Having crises and flirting with failure is not easy for a 20-something person. But if the worst comes to the worst, they can start again a little older and much wiser. Doing an MBA is a safe and prestigious way for a 20-something person to start over again. In contrast, the 40-year-old who has never had a crisis has what one CEO called 'brittle' confidence – they look good, sound good and seem confident. But when they face a real challenge or crisis, they crumble. They have no reserves to call on. They make a sad sight as they justify why they are happy to be leaving the rat race and how they had always dreamed of pig farming.

Many graduate training programmes do not develop resilience. They test the graduate's appetite for hard work, but that is not the same as resilience. Teach First is an exception. Top graduates spend two years teaching in some of the most challenging schools in the UK. This is, potentially, a brutal experience. But these graduates develop a depth of confidence, resilience and people skills that can never be acquired by their better-paid peers who spend their first two years staring into computer screens trading bonds or doing research. Leaders of the future need to take risks and learn about adversity and resilience early in the careers. Trying to learn these things when you are 40-something is tough.

The leaders who talked about responding to crises talked about the importance of knowing yourself. Some people let their identity become swamped by their job. When the crisis hits, or when they retire, they have nothing to fall back on. They have become dependent on their job – they live to work. Nearly all the leaders I interviewed had active lives outside work. This gives them a level of independence that makes them better able to deal with challenges.

Ultimately, individuals need to know themselves. Leadership is not for everyone, nor is it necessary for everyone. If you prefer fishing, then focus on that.

Risks

Attitudes to risk and ambiguity are the acid test for differentiating leaders, managers and entrepreneurs.

Risk and ambiguity are kryptonite to managers. They want to create an orderly environment in which predetermined goals can be achieved by the organization. These are extremely valuable skills to have in an organization. If everyone was a risk and ambiguity junkie, you would either have an extremely dysfunctional organization or you would have an investment bank. In some cases, you would have an extremely dysfunctional investment bank. But if an organization takes no risk and avoids all ambiguity, it will eventually go nowhere fast.

I learned the value of risk when I learned skiing. We were all stuck on the nursery slopes being told being told to 'bend zee knees'. After we had mastered a cautious snowplough turn, we were encouraged to try for more ambitious and professional turns. After falling over six or seven times, most of us stuck to the safety of the snowplough turn. One maniac persisted with trying the fancy turns. He became the group joker; he was always falling over to the amusement of everyone else. Towards the end of the week, we all stopped laughing. He had slowly mastered the fancy turns and proceeded to start doing all the more adventurous runs we could only dream of. He left us far behind in ability. Most of us were acting like managers. We were avoiding risk. The embryonic leader was taking risks, learning and developing far faster than we were. We had learned survival. He had learned success.

Leaders will take risks, will persist and will achieve mastery through experience. As they build experience, they build skill and confidence. There is, inevitably, a risk/reward trade-off that we all think about. Most people are risk averse. The fear of failure outweighs the uncertain possibilities of success. Leaders tend to think more positively about the risk return trade-off, and enjoy accelerated careers as a result: they succeed fast or they fail fast.

Although leaders take risks, most leaders try to minimize ambiguity and uncertainty. Oil exploration, pharmaceutical R&D and insurance are all risk-based industries. Billions of dollars may be at risk. Although the leaders must make billion-dollar bets, they will seek to create as much clarity and certainty around those choices as possible. Good risk-taking is gambling where the dice are as loaded as far as possible in your favour.

Rewards for the leader in the middle of the matrix are not just about completing the project, getting a promotion or bonus. Those are short-term rewards that are soon forgotten. Long-term rewards are more important. Typically, there are four questions to address:

▶ Does this opportunity help me build skills which are useful in future?
▶ Am I set up for success or failure?

▶ Is there sufficient recognition and reward for taking this risk?

▶ Are the consequences of failure manageable?

In other words, the leader in the middle has to make a calculated gamble on the career consequences of taking any risk. In any organization there are CLMs (Career Limiting Moves) which everyone informally recognizes. These include working for the wrong boss or working on the wrong assignment or in the wrong part of the organization.

For the emerging leader, the greatest risk of all is to take no risk. Avoiding risk is a career survival decision. But survival and success are not the same thing. To succeed, you need to take risks.

The entrepreneur is also a leader. Aspiring leaders in established organizations can learn from entrepreneurs' attitudes to risk and ambiguity. They are the opposite of what the institutional leader would do. Most entrepreneurs see ambiguity as opportunity. Where the rules of the game are unclear, the entrepreneur will create the rules of the game, even if this means making them up as they go along. Charlie Dunstone (mobile telephones), Michael O'Leary (discount airlines) and Richard Branson (everything else) did not wait for the rules of their industries to be written before attacking them. They entered, created their own rules and won. It is easier to win a game when you write the rules for it.

Managing projects

Project management versus change management

Change management and project management are the bread and butter of leaders in the middle of the matrix. Change and project management are often talked of as if they are the same thing. They are not. Project management is the technical, task-focused subset of change management. Projects focus on who does what where, when and how. For the sake of focus here, we will assume that change management includes project management but looks much more at the human, political and emotional aspects of change. Change is not simply about setting goals and drawing up a plan in an office. It is about creating the alliances, support and power networks to enable the plan to happen. This is a skill which all leaders acquire and use. Most CEOs do not rely on command and control to get their way. They spend much of their time working the levers of the organization to make things happen. They use influence and persuasion as much as formal power.

Good project management is the hallmark of a good manager. The manager delivers against preordained goals with preordained resources. Good change management is the hallmark of the good leader. The leader goes beyond formal authority, using influencing and political skills effectively, to make things happen.

The contrast between change and project management became clear in a merger. The two sides of the merger brought in some consultants to help, which is always a dangerous idea. The partner did what the board needed: he acted as a leader. Although he had no formal authority, he convened the executive committee on a daily basis and helped them work through the daily crises, which happen in any merger. Behind the scenes, he worked the politics of the individuals involved. The consultants then put in a team to project manage the merger integration. After ten days, they had established a war room with risk logs and issue logs (spot the difference, if you can), meeting logs, attendance logs, telephone logs and master logs. Everything was being logged, and nothing was being done. The client went crazy. Logs and paper do not change things, people do. They tried to manage change: you have to lead change.

However, leaders also have to deliver the basics of project management as well. We will look at effective project and change management below.

The basics of project management

Good project management is a real skill and it is in short supply. Projects have a nasty habit of taking twice as long and costing twice as much as the original bid. Anyone who has had building work done knows this, to their cost. Some projects go completely out of control. The Scottish Parliament escalated in price from an initial £10–20 millon bid to over £400 million. Politicians may be great leaders. They are rarely good managers.

❝ *Good project management is a real skill and it is in short supply.* **❞**

Here we will not focus on the vagaries of contract management. One reason contractors cost more than you thought is that they underbid in the first place. Either they were too optimistic, or they hoped to make up their loss on all the changes and additions that are inevitably requested in the course of any project, from building a new kitchen to building a new CRM database.

There are exhaustive manuals on how to run tight projects. We will focus on the few items which make the big difference. Most projects, like most battles, are decided before they really start. In the middle of the matrix, it pays to make sure that your projects are set up for success, not failure.

Project management hell is brought about by the four horsemen of project apocalypse:

1 The wrong problem
2 The wrong sponsor
3 The wrong team
4 The wrong process

Get these wrong, and your project is doomed. Get them right, and it takes a stroke of evil genius to make it go wrong. Figure 6.1 illustrates where leaders focus their efforts on projects: at the start, before the heavy lifting begins.

Figure 6.1 Projects: effort and potential to influence the outcome

We will take a look at each of the four horsemen of the apocalypse.

The wrong problem

There is a story of a drunk who loses his car keys in a dark alley. He can't see anything there, so he goes into the main street where there is plenty of street lighting and looks for his car keys there. He figures that at least he can see what he is looking for there. Too many managers look where it is easy, not where it is useful. To be useful, we must look in the right area and solve the right problem, even when it is difficult.

There are many experts who know the answer. They are like solutions drifting across the business world in search of a problem to which they can attach themselves. Their pitch is as beguiling as that of the quack doctors in the Wild West selling their miracle cure-all medicines. Because they offer an easy answer, often management leaps aboard the band wagon. A good answer is useless if it answers the wrong problem. '42' is a good answer to 'What it six times seven?' It is also, for some people, a good answer to 'What is the meaning of life?' It is not such a good answer to 'What is the capital of Croatia?'

Finding the right problem is not easy. We are offered cost cutting, re-engineering, supply chain management, service excellence and all manner of initiatives. In all cases, repeatedly asking 'why' helps. For instance, a hotel manager wanted to raise room rates. We started to ask why. We took a couple of weeks of digging around to find the data which produced this logic flow:

We must raise room rates	Why?
We must improve profits	Why?
Because profits are down	Why?
Our costs per customer are up	Why?
We are getting fewer customers	Why?
Competitors charge less than us	So...
We should reduce room rates	

Naturally, the logic flow does not drop out quite as simply as that. It might take anything from a few minutes to a few months to tease out the logic flow. In this case, the logic flow encouraged the hotel manager to take exactly the opposite action from his first intention: he cut room rates instead of raising them.

The wrong sponsor

There is an easy way of finding the right problem – find the right sponsor. Consultants love working for chief executives, for several reasons.

- ▶ You always get paid.
- ▶ The CEO has the power and authority to make things happen and can cut through political log jams.
- ▶ A CEO project always succeeds. Even if it fails, it will still be made to look like a success in public.

It is possible that the CEO is solving the wrong problem. In practice, there is often a conspiracy of silence that lets the CEO plough on in the wrong direction. Challenging the CEO is a dangerous sport. You may land up becoming highly trusted and valued for your insight and honesty. You may land up doing the corporate equivalent of cleaning toilets in Siberia.

Not all projects are CEO projects, but the same characteristics are required of a good sponsor:

- ▶ The project should be a 'must-win' battle for the future personal success of the sponsor. You want a sponsor who is totally committed to success. Otherwise, you suffer asymmetric risk: you take the risk of failure while the sponsor walks away, or the sponsor claims the credit if you succeed.
- ▶ The sponsor must have the power and influence to be able to overcome all the political log jams that occur on any project.
- ▶ The sponsor has to have enough authority and resources to enable the project to happen.

The wrong team

Inevitably, the people you want on a project team are not available. If people are good, then they are fully committed elsewhere. The only people who are available are the people sitting on the beach, waiting to become fully utilized. They are typically a mix of the untried and untested, together with a few who have been tried, tested and have not covered themselves in glory. Even if some good people are available, they may well not have the particular technical skills that are important for the success of your project.

At this point, the successful project manager should play hard ball. Accepting the B team is a recipe for B-grade results, long nights, crises and frustration.

A good way of testing how important a project is, is to see who is placed on to the project team. If the sponsor and CEO are happy to see a B team on the project, they clearly regard it as a B-type priority. This is a good time to walk away from the project. If they are prepared to make sacrifices and release the A-team players from their other commitments, then clearly they regard the project as having A-grade priority.

The wrong process

Of the four horsemen of project apocalypse, this is the least dangerous. It is also where project management manuals focus all their attention. But if you have the right problem, sponsor and team then the odds are heavily stacked in your favour. The chances are that you will already have the right process. Even if it turns out to be the wrong process, you have enough fire power in the team to correct your course.

Beyond the elaborate world of GANTT charts and PERT charts, there are three basics to the right process:

- ▶ Start at the end, and work backwards.
- ▶ Figure out the minimum number of steps required to get there.
- ▶ Create an effective governance process.

Starting at the start is never a good idea. Define the end outcome as clearly as possible before the start so that everyone knows where they are heading. Knowing the destination minimizes the risks of deviations en route and cost escalations from contractors.

66 Define the end outcome as clearly as possible before the start so that everyone knows where they are heading. 99

If you know the end point, then figure out the minimum number of steps required to get there. There are always staffers who can discover bottomless pits of detail to fall into. The challenge for the leader is to make it simple so that everyone stays focused on what is really important.

By looking for the minimum number of steps, the project manager should also be defining the critical path (what events need to happen before others can be started) and will also make it much easier to control and monitor progress.

Effective governance is essential. A good way to escalate costs and time is to change your mind frequently and make decisions slowly. This happens often where there is a political environment and not all the constituencies are truly aligned. Clear goals and clear decision-making processes are vital. The other governance trap is to have no governance: many projects are started but have no effective follow-through from top management. A strong leader in the middle of the matrix will insist on continued oversight from top management. This helps when it comes to keeping the project on track and overcoming obstacles. It also helps maintain the visibility of the project. A successful project which is invisible to top management does not help its leader much.

Managing change

Many people think that projects exist in the rational world of GANTT charts, progress meetings and task groups. Anyone who has breathed air in an organization will know that organizations are highly political. Organizations are also full of people. Unlike computers, most people have emotions. So projects do not live on a purely rational planet all of their own. They live in a world which is:

- ▶ rational
- ▶ political
- ▶ emotional.

The assiduous project manager will work in the rational world of the project. The change leader will work with the political and emotional agendas of colleagues to effect change and to assure the success of diverse projects.

'Working the political and emotional agendas' sounds very vague and slightly undoable. Much of it does come down to experience, which does not help much if you don't have the experience. Even if you do have the experience, it pays to have something more structured than your innate genius and intuition to rely on when it comes to making change. What worked last time may not work in different circumstances this time.

In practice, there are three tools that can help a leader in the middle of the matrix maximize the chances of success in dealing with change:

1   Setting up change to succeed.

2   Managing the change process.

3   Managing the change network.

Setting up change to succeed

Most sane people do not enjoy change. Change implies uncertainty and risk. Even if I can succeed currently, how do I know that I can succeed in a new environment with a new boss doing new things? The less control over the change I have, the more I am likely to fear it. So change is dominated by the FUD factor:

- ▶ Fear

- ▶ Uncertainty

- ▶ Doubt.

The only people who do not suffer from the FUD factor are CEOs, senior leaders and consultants. They are able to control the change, and they know how they intend to benefit from it.

Over the years, one simple formula has been a constant predictor of change success or failure. Here it is, in all its spurious mathematical accuracy:

$$V + N + C + F \geq R$$

$V = Vision$. This is not a 'save the planet' type vision. It is a worthwhile goal which convinces people that the destination is a good one, and that they have a role to play in it. The vision has to mean something to the organization, to the team and to each individual. Increasing Earnings Per Share is pretty meaningless to a shop floor worker.

$N = Need$. There has to be a perceived need to change, both for the institution and the individual. The risks of doing nothing must outweigh the risks of doing something. Fear is often a powerful motivator for change. Leaders at all levels often find themselves spending much of their time selling both their vision and the need to change to the organization.

C = Capacity to change. It is no use having both the vision and the need if the organization lacks the skills or resources to change. Individuals want to know that they can make the journey from today to tomorrow successfully. They also need to trust management. If management announces a new five-year plan every six months, then the next five-year plan is likely to be greeted with some cynicism.

F = First steps. We live in a world of instant gratification. We want to know that we are backing a winner. The smart change leader recognizes this and will seek out some early wins – some early signs of success that will bring all the doubters and fence sitters on board.

R= Risks and costs of change. The risks and costs to the organization can normally be dealt with fairly rationally. The killer risks are the emotional and political risks to individuals and departments, who all suffer the FUD factor in change. A large part of the leader's role in leading change is to de-risk the perceived risk of the change. The rational risks can be mitigated rationally: phasing investments to minimize exposure, testing ideas, prototyping and so forth. The FUD factor will often be hidden behind rational reasons. When people don't want to do something, they become very creative and articulate in discovering rational reasons why they should not do it. The effective leader will see past this rational veil to the political and emotional concerns involved. Working in private the leader will seek to reduce the FUD factor, typically in three ways:

▶ Try to align the vision of the change with the personal vision and expectations of the other person or department. Find common ground.

▶ Try to alter the perceived risk of doing nothing versus changing. Increasing the fear of inaction is effective although unkind.

▶ Give the other people a sense of involvement or control over the change. Simply asking for their advice helps allay their concerns and makes them feel less threatened.

As a leader, it pays to work the whole agenda. Constantly remind people of the vision and relate it to their needs. Build up the need to change and the risks of doing nothing. Find some early successes to keep people encouraged, and make sure that there is enough capacity to support the change. All of this needs to be balanced against risk reduction: few people truly enjoy risk. The greater the perceived risk, the greater the resistance to change. Make the change very low risk, and no one will get in your way.

Managing the change process

Project managers can manage the technical and rational aspects of change. The change leader needs to manage the political and emotional consequences of change. Most significant change programmes go through a predictable emotional and political cycle, outlined in Figure 6.2.

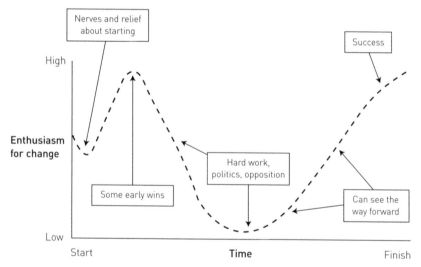

Figure 6.2 Change and the valley of death

If the change leader has used the change equation successfully, then there will be some early enthusiasm for change. Some early wins bring more of the doubters on board, and everything starts to look good. It is at this point that things start to go wrong. After the initial flush of enthusiasm dies away, slowly people start to understand the scale of the change required. They start to see the logical consequences of change: the exciting vision of the change painted by the leader becomes obscured by the reality of the effort and risks involved. There is rarely one event that triggers collapse. Usually the change slowly meanders into a swamp of despair.

The fair weather friends that hopped on board at the first sign of success are hopping off at the first sign of trouble. They now create distance between themselves and your change. They may offer advice, but it is poisoned advice. Take the advice and then they will claim they turned the programme around. Refuse the advice and they will have the ammunition to show that you failed because you refused the advice. Suddenly, you can start to feel very lonely and very beleaguered.

Inevitably, prevention is better than cure for the mid-life crises of change. If you have put in the right preconditions for success, both in terms of project management and in terms of the change agenda, you will pull through. If the change was started prematurely, you may fail. There will not be enough belief in the vision or enough political support to overcome the opposition to change.

Curiously, the valley of death is essential to most successful change programmes. It is only in the valley of death that people fully realize the scale of the change they will need to make. Opposition to change is the surest sign that they are at last taking the change seriously, that they are engaged. So a leader should not avoid the valley of death: they should seek it out.

In most major changes I have started, I have alerted the client or the sponsor to the change cycle and the valley of death at the start. If they know it is coming, they worry about it less: they realize it is natural and are ready to work through it. In several cases the CEO has kept on asking, like a child on a long journey, 'Are we there yet? Is this it? Have we got to the valley of death yet?' As a rule, you have not arrived in the valley of death until you find yourself uttering the words 'This is the worst I have ever seen'. This is when everyone is really grasping reality.

In the valley of death, followers give up. Leaders look to the future; they keep their eyes fixed on the end goal and figure out the way of getting there. At a time when everyone else is seeing problems, the leader stands out by offering solutions and actions. In this slough of despond, people want solutions. For the leader, the valley of death is a moment of truth: it is when they prove their capability and it tends to be when they learn and develop the most.

If all this does is to give you some hope next time your change effort hits crisis, then it has at least done some good. Remember, the difference between success and failure is often no more than persistence.

Managing the change network

There is one big catch in setting up change to succeed. Leaders often want everyone to join their jolly bandwagon. Normally, this is not possible. There will always be some diehards who would resist anything. The successful change network consists of those people who collectively have the power, skills and resources to assure the success of the change. In addition, the change leader needs the critical mass of the organization to be supportive. It is a trap to try to engage the whole organization. The challenge can be seen in Figure 6.3.

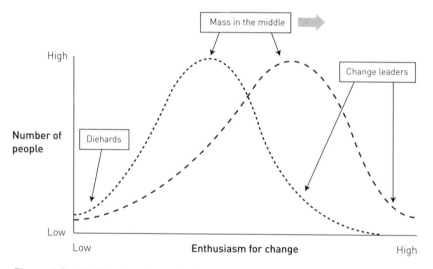

Figure 6.3   Shifting the change bell curve

This diagram shows that most people feel pretty indifferent to the idea of change in principle. In practice, their enthusiasm will wax and wane depending where they are in the valley of death. But the bell curve effect will always be present.

There are always extremes at each end of the change bell curve. At one end are the change enthusiasts who can be recruited as the active leaders and early adopters of change. At the other end, some will always resist. Do not waste time on them. Let them see that the change is succeeding, and let them make up their own minds. They will start to feel lonely, left on the platform after the change train moves off. They can decide to leave or get on board. And if they want to protest by lying down on the tracks in front of the train, let them know the train will not stop anyway. The change resistors can consume a disproportionate amount of management time and effort. In practice, management needs to move the mass of people from neutrality to mild acceptance of change. Again, do not expect everyone to become change enthusiasts.

At one chemicals company, the plant manager was very frustrated that he could not implement a new set of working practices. We were asked to help. We soon heard loud objections to the whole change idea, expressed very forcibly. They used every reason to object: from cost to work–life balance to health and safety to threats of walk outs. But we found the objections were all coming from a small group of staff and managers in the power plant. Most other people were quietly supportive, but felt overawed by the loud-mouthed middle managers. And the plant manager had let himself become hostage to them – they had secured an effective veto over his plans. Instead of focusing on the objectors, we focused on the supporters. As we started to implement the changes in the more supportive areas, people realized they liked the changes and became bolder about supporting them. We did not need to negotiate with the objectors: one by one they made their own decisions. Some got with the programme, some got out. As a change leader, do not try to please all the people all the time: you will get nowhere.

Aside from the mass of people, the change leader needs to worry acutely about building the right power network in support of change. Building networks and alliances is essential to the leader in the middle of the matrix, and is the subject of the next section.

Building power, influence and networks

The days of command and control are long gone. The flat organization may lead to empowerment, but it also leads to dispersal of power. The leader in the middle of the matrix has more responsibility than authority, so can only achieve things through influence, alliances and networks. It takes time to build the trust and knowledge on which these networks are built. Often, leaders only find out how subtle and important these networks are when they fall prey to the headhunter's siren calls. The leader who has operated very effectively in one organization is tempted to the greener grass in another organization. When they move, they suddenly discover that they do not have the influence and networks on which they relied in the past; they do not even know which are the critical levers to pull in order to make things happen. Leadership is very often context specific. The heroic leader that leaps from one organization to the next, putting out fires and transforming frogs into princes is a rare beast. Most effective leaders are creatures of their organizations. They have learned how to make things happen.

This section is about making things happen through networks. It addresses two main issues:

1   What is the network a leader needs to build?
2   How do you build an influencing network?

Networking and alliance management are two more ways to differentiate between managers and leaders. Managers will work comfortably within their sphere of authority. Leaders will seek to build alliances, networks and influence that enable them to achieve more than their formal authority would seem to indicate.

What is the network a leader needs to build?

Organizations have formal power structures which are well known. Leaders need to tap into the informal power network, which is at least as important when it comes to making things happen.

❝ In the complicated world of the matrix, it pays to achieve simplicity and clarity. ❞

In the complicated world of the matrix, it pays to achieve simplicity and clarity. At the risk of being trite and over-simplistic, here is a simple acronym to help figure out the network the leader needs: GRANTS.

Gatekeepers
Resources
Authorizers
Network nodes
Technical influencers
Sponsors

To make the simple complicated for a moment, we will start at the end. Each part of the network can offer you different things, and each looks for different things in return. It is worth remembering that this is a business network, not a social network. They are colleagues first. If they are friends, that is useful but secondary. Remember the dictum of Benjamin Disraeli, the nineteenth-century British prime minister: 'Nations have no permanent friends or enemies. They only have permanent interests.' The business leader rarely has permanent friends *or* permanent enemies.

Sponsors are essential for career survival and success. They are probably not your immediate boss. Hopefully, they are at least one level above that. A good sponsor is a power figure in the organization who can act as your mentor, coach and occasional political fixer. When you are faced with the potential of an impossible assignment with an impossible boss, this is the time to cash in your chips with the sponsor and find a way of dodging the bullet coming your way. There is an informal psychological contract with the sponsor: you make yourself useful to the sponsor through odd jobs and useful information about what is happening. The sponsor then looks out for your interests in return.

Authorizers are your boss or bosses. The rules of managing up to bosses have been covered earlier in Chapter 1. Ultimately, loyalty is prized above all, and then performance. Although they have authority over you, they do not have the authority to help you achieve all you need to achieve; you need your own network for this.

Resources are the people and skills at your disposal. Again, they are unlikely to represent all that you need to accomplish all your goals. An effective leader will also leverage resources throughout the rest of the organization by begging, borrowing and stealing them. They will make alliances with other authorizers or resource holders to work on a common agenda. We will cover the process of influence building in the next section. More traditional managers will try to do it by themselves with their own resources: this lack of leverage and support makes achieving the best outcome practically and politically nearly impossible, while also consigning the managers to many late nights and high stress.

Technical influencers are essential to success. They lack much formal authority, although informally they have power of veto over things. The classic technical influencer is the finance department. They look over proposals and check that they are fit and proper. If they are not on your side, they can destroy any proposal you have. Make friends with them early. Comply without complaint with their unreasonable demands. Involve them early in your proposal and actively seek their advice in shaping your idea; they will be flattered that you value them. Finance are the sheriffs that keep order in town. As any cowboy knows, you can really have fun when the sheriff is on your side.

Network nodes seem to know all the right people. They may have little formal authority themselves. Perhaps a few key executives share a common personal coach. Or there is an old-timer in HR or another staff function that everyone trusts: he is going nowhere and has no ambition but is seen as absolutely trustworthy. Because they are seen to be above the political fray, these people's views often carry weight. They also tend to be very well informed because everyone talks to them. This naturally makes them even better informed, so even more people talk to them. Find these people, find what makes them tick and bring them on board.

Gatekeepers can be very useful or very damaging. A good gatekeeper can help you gain access to executives who are hard to get to. A poor gatekeeper will promise access and will turn out to be either unwilling or unable to gain you access; you will have wasted valuable time not getting to the right people. The most obvious gatekeepers are secretaries. People tend to mistreat them in at least one of three ways:

▶ Ignoring them or using them as door mats on the road to power.

▶ Treating them as servants and ordering them around.

▶ Condescending to them: flowers, chocolates and long conversations may be fine for lovers, but most secretaries like to be seen for what they are: skilled professionals doing a good job. Treat them that way, and they will treat you well in return.

In addition to this influencing network there are the power barons who have the real authority to make things happen. It is tempting to do an 'end run' and go straight to the power baron for help. There are three problems with this:

▶ The power baron may have authority, but will still want to see that the rest of the organization supports the way forward. If the informal influencers and technical influencers are whispering in the baron's ear against you, you are dead meat.

▶ The influencing network will hate you for going around them, so they will probably whisper bad things to the power baron.

▶ Even if the baron supports you, making things happen by saying 'It's what the baron wants' is very weak and will discredit you hugely in the longer term. You have become little more than the baron's gofer and will be left out in the cold when the baron moves on.

How do you build an influencing network?

You build a network the same way you build a wall: one brick at a time. It takes time and care. Each alliance with each individual in the network will be based on a slightly different psychological contract. At the heart of this contract is the Trust Equation. As individuals, we are prepared to support and follow people we trust. Certainly, we do not follow people we do not trust. Trust is the basic currency of any alliance.

The Trust Equation is simple to describe but hard to fulfil. Once again risking spurious mathematical accuracy, here is the Trust Equation:

$$T = (I \times C) \div R$$

$T = Trust$. The more mutual trust there is, the more the degree of mutual influence.

$I = Intimacy$, but not in the normal sense of the word. Although getting into bed with the boss has a long and ignoble history of success, you make your own decision on that. Intimacy here means having the same set of values and interests: we both talk the same language, see the world the same way and share some common goals and interests. This intimacy comes from spending time with people and listening to them. The more you listen, the more you understand and the more they will appreciate you.

Executives often leave clues to let you establish intimacy, even when you have never met. Photographs are a giveaway. Pictures of houses and cars (ask about them – probably their pride and joy); pictures of football teams (commiserate with them for supporting a team like Spurs); pictures of lakes (ask them about their holidays). Once you have a mutual interest, you have the chance of building mutual understanding. If there are no pictures on the wall or mementoes on the table, you may have a hard ass who just wants to get down to business.

C= Credibility. If intimacy means talking the talk, then credibility is about walking the walk. You have to be able to deliver on what you say. If you are all talk and no action, you are little more than an amusing irritant. Think of it as building up personal equity. Each time you deliver on something which is of interest to the other person, your personal stock rises. Each time you need a favour in return, you are drawing on your equity. It pays to keep a mildly positive balance. If you are always doing things for someone, they may well take you for granted. It needs to be a partnership in which they commit time and effort as much as you do.

R= Risk. Our old friend risk is never far away. We may trust strangers and new employees with trivial tasks. But the more important the task, the deeper the trust has to be. Building trust takes time. We have to earn our spurs and show that we can be trusted on ever more challenging and risky assignments.

Clearly, this Trust Equation will be at different stages of development with different individuals. As a leader, you need some way of accelerating this network development.

A quick way to gain trust is to go to the bank and borrow it. You may need to build trust and influence with someone you do not know well in the organization. But the chances are that they know someone who knows you. If that person is a strong supporter of you, then that reference will carry credibility with the other person. One of the best fund raisers I ever met would spend the first 15 minutes of a meeting with a new prospect just talking about potential mutual acquaintances. Soon enough, the two strangers would figure out that they knew several people in common. They would talk about them glowingly. Inside 15 minutes, they would have got themselves onto the first rung of mutual trust, despite never having met before. Once they had some element of trust, the fund raiser could start to talk about business.

There is one final trick the leader needs to play to build an alliance in a hurry. It is something that all good entrepreneurs know how to do instinctively. They create a sense of inevitability about what they will do. They don't use *if*, they use *when*. They talk up the level of support and commitment they have. If finance are still looking at the proposal with a fine-tooth comb, then they 'are deeply involved with the programme and helping position it right'. Entrepreneurs create a huge sense of enthusiasm around the vision they have and deliberately make light of the risks and challenges. When I decided to start a bank, with neither the skills nor the money, I approached potential partners with the total conviction that the bank would happen. The only questions were who would be lucky enough to be my partner, and who would lose out on the huge opportunity. If you do not believe in yourself, no one else will.

7

Being professional

By the time that leaders finally emerge from the ranks of bright-eyed graduates, they have probably become thoroughly domesticated animals. They have learned the behavioural norms of the organization. They have learned some craft and trade skills in their industry; they know how to trade bonds or cut code. They have performed well enough to get promoted. They are converting the potential of future leaders into the reality of current leadership.

So it seems unfair to suggest that the matrix professional needs to learn how to be professional. Membership of the matrix implies that a basic standard of professionalism has already been achieved. The situation is like that of the medieval guilds. The apprenticeship has been served, but the apprentice is not yet ready to become the master. In between the apprentice and the master is the journeyman, who hones and develops the basic skills en route to becoming the master.

For the matrix leader, professionalism is a mix of behaviours and skills. Professional behaviours are about demonstrating the values of a real leader and being a role model for others. Many people fail both at this level and at the top leadership level because they have failed to develop some of the core behaviours of successful leaders. If you do not develop them at this level, it is too late to hope that they will suddenly emerge at the top of the organization.

Essential behaviours include things such as honesty and integrity. Honesty and integrity in leadership terms have nothing to do with ethics, and nothing to do with preaching from the pulpit about being a nice person. For the leader, honesty and integrity are about survival, not ethics. This is covered in more detail in Chapter 11 on top leadership. But the core of the argument is simple. Think of the people you are prepared to follow. How many of them lie to you or withhold the truth from you? Followers demand leaders they can trust who tell them the whole truth. If you are less than honest, you have no followers. A leader without any followers is a very sad creature.

❝ Followers demand leaders they can trust who tell them the whole truth. If you are less than honest, you have no followers. ❞

At this point, take a deep breath and sit down. You are going to be asked to emulate the White Queen in *Alice's Adventures In Wonderland* who claimed 'sometimes I've believed as many as six impossible things before breakfast'. Below are six impossible things for you to believe before you proceed any further into the leadership journey:

1 We do not know how to talk.

2 We do not know how to listen.

3 We do not know how to write.

4 We do not know how to read.

5 We do not know how to meet.

6 We do not know how to communicate.

The list looks absurd. Of course, we all know how to read, write, talk and listen. We do it every day. So let's take a step back. *You* know how to read, write, talk and listen. But how about your colleagues? How much turgid drivel do you have to wade through in their e-mails, PowerPoint presentations and Word documents? How often have you been to conferences where some important panjandrum gets on stage and drones on at you, communicating nothing except his self-importance? Have you noticed how colleagues often don't get the message, even when you have communicated clearly with them in writing and in person? There is plenty of evidence that no one else can read, write, talk or listen.

At this point, the leader in the matrix should learn that an essential professional behaviour is humility. Humility is the gateway to self-awareness, learning and improved performance. The humble leader will always seek to improve their core communication skills. We spend most of our day talking, listening, reading or writing. It pays to be good at what you do all day.

We need to recognize that the core skills of reading, writing, talking and listening are fundamentally different in the social and managerial worlds. The ineffective professional recognizes this and responds by creating ponderous documents full of management speak. This is meant to make them look serious. The jargon-filled documents and speeches then fail in their core mission, which is to communicate.

The effective leader learns how to communicate effectively in an organization. Good communication reflects good thinking, and is the hallmark of many strong leaders, from Churchill to Reagan.

Below we look at the six impossible things we have been asked to believe. For each one, we look at how communicating in the managerial and social worlds are different and at how to become more effective. Each one of these skills areas can take a lifetime to learn. Strong leaders experiment, reflect and develop a style which suits them. The notes below are simply a way of helping structure and accelerate that journey of discovery.

Learning how to talk

The Bambara are the largest farming tribe in Mali. They are largely illiterate. But they regard words as being close to gods. Words create whole new worlds in the mind; words make people do things; words separate humans from beasts. Words are powerful. The Bambara say that words should be forged like a blacksmith, woven like a weaver, and polished like a cobbler. Not surprisingly, they value restraint in how people talk – better to talk little and well than to talk for the sake of it.

Words can have as much power in the management tribe as they can in the Bambara tribe. We cover the art of communicating, motivating, influencing and coaching one-to-one in other chapters. Here we will look at the specific challenge of talking to large groups. For emerging leaders these showpiece events can have a disproportionate influence on how they are perceived. Some people are terrified of such events. The people who think that they are born demagogues are often even worse.

The art of effective presentation can be split into two parts:

1 Substance
2 Style

Effective speaking: substance

The ancient Greeks lived in a direct democracy. There were no representatives: every adult Greek male (women, slaves, lunatics and prisoners did not count in this curious democracy) could vote. Power was vested with the leader who could speak best and sway the citizens with the force of argument. Pericles came close to ruling Athens as an autocrat through the power of his speaking. Thucydides said that if Pericles was beaten in a wrestling contest he would stand up and be able to convince all the on-lookers that he had just won.

For the Greeks, the art of speaking came down to three things: logos, ethos and pathos.

Logos is about logic. It answers the question 'Why should I listen to this?' Good speakers quickly answer the question 'Why should I listen to this?' In simple terms they say what they are going to say, say it and then say that they have said it. Instead of telling a joke rather badly to start a speech, tell people why they should listen. If it is a large group, do not try to speak to everyone. There are probably just a few people in the audience you really want to influence. Maybe there is only one person you need to influence. Speak to that person.

Ethos answers the question 'Why do I believe this person?' You need to establish your credentials fast. This is not just about showing that you are expert. It is about showing that you can connect with the issues that concern your audience, you can relate to their experience and talk to them at a level and in a way that they will appreciate.

Pathos builds the emotional connection with the audience. The speaker who relies on the relentless logic of spreadsheets and detail will quickly lose the audience. Effective pathos requires bringing the logic to life through telling relevant stories and using vivid illustrations. Everyone likes stories, and these can be good ways of conveying difficult messages.

Effective speaking: style

❝ An audience is more likely to remember you than your message; in many ways, you are the message. ❞

It is a truism that an audience is more likely to remember you than your message; in many ways, you are the message. So if you are the king of the mumblers, dress like a tramp and slouch like a teenager in full hormonal angst, the chances are that the brilliance of your message will be lost on the audience. In contrast, if you can remember the three *E*s of communication, even a dull message is likely to come across well:

▶ Energy

▶ Enthusiasm

▶ Excitement.

It is as hard to fake these three *E*s as it is to rehearse spontaneity. But there are some things that can help. Some of the *dos* include:

▶ Throw away the script. With it, you will sound wooden or, worse, like a politician. Instead, memorize your opening so that you can make a good start. Memorize your conclusion so that you can make a good finish. Memorize some choice phrases that you want to insert on your way through; each phrase is a waymarker on your speech. You will keep your structure and discipline while sounding spontaneous.

▶ Avoid complicated slide presentations. If you have slides, the principle is to have dumb slides but a smart presenter. The slide might have three or four key words to help the audience anchor where you are – you provide the commentary. The nightmare is to have smart slides which explain everything and a dumb presenter who reads the slides more slowly than the audience.

▶ Stand on the front of your feet, so that a slip of paper could pass under your heel. Weight on the back of the foot encourages slouching and lower your energy.

▶ Try to stand before going on stage. If you are sitting down before speaking, all your energy is down. You are likely to overcompensate with a sudden rush of adrenalin.

▶ Engage the audience. Look individuals in the eye, rather than gazing into the middle distance. Billy Graham, the great American preacher, did this with devastating effect. Even in an audience of a thousand, he would pick out individuals and catch their eye for a moment or two. No one dared doze off and they felt that they were being addressed personally.

The three *E*s are greatly enhanced by two more *E*s: expertise and enjoyment. If you are expert at your subject, you are more likely to relax and enjoy what you are saying. If you are enjoying it, your audience is likely to enjoy it as well. If you hate it, do not expect the audience to enjoy it. As an experiment, try telling someone about how the cost allocation system in your organization works. See if you fall asleep before your audience does. Now try recounting one of the most memorable events in your personal or professional life. You will naturally display all five *E*s: energy, enthusiasm, excitement, expertise and enjoyment. Such a simple exercise shows that we can all speak well – we simply have to transfer our skills on to the big stage.

Learning how to listen

It had been a very good meeting with the client. Paula was surprised – she had been expecting it to be something of a disaster. The client had a reputation as a hard ass. She turned to James, the partner in charge, and said, 'That was great. How did you do it? You looked like you were really interested in what the client was saying. You made him feel like he was the only person that counted in the world.'

Good listening is devastatingly effective. Like sincerity and spontaneity, it is difficult to fake. Good salespeople and good leaders, like most normal people, have one mouth and two ears and they use them in that proportion. People like listening to the one person they truly trust and admire: themselves. Give people the chance, and they will talk themselves into submission.

Each of the following three cases includes two approaches. Think about which approach is likely to be more effective in each case.

▶ *The sales call.* Spend 15 minutes telling your client about the wonders of new miracle Sudso, which cleans up the competition, and then ask for the sale. Naturally, the client will find a thousand objections and, at best, negotiate like crazy on price. Or let the client talk about their competitive situation, and direct your questions to helping them focus on the sorts of challenges miracle Sudso happens to address. They will discover that they need Sudso and you can be their partner in solving their problem. You have moved from being a salesperson to a partner.

▶ *The staff challenge.* Your staff bring you a problem. You are the heroic leader who is the fountain of all knowledge, so you solve their problem and tell them exactly what to do. They leave the room feeling that you are clever, but they have no ownership over the solution. And they have learned dependence: it is easier to bring problems to you than it is to solve them themselves. Or you ask questions, let them figure out the answer, let them own both the problem and the solution, to which they are now committed because they feel it is their idea.

▶ *The performance review.* Tell the staff member that they are underperforming; be clear about what has gone wrong and what remedial action is expected. Watch them retreat, depressed or angry or in denial. Alternatively, let them talk through their performance. Ask questions to make them focus on what they can do better and how they can do better. Watch them leave, feeling cautiously optimistic that they have a way forward. They will also feel grateful and loyal to a boss who has listened and cared.

“ *There are three fairly straightforward things you can do to develop listening skills, apart from putting tape across your mouth.* **”**

Listening is much more difficult than talking. Active listening requires acute thinking and acute questioning. There are three fairly straightforward things you can do to develop listening skills, apart from putting tape across your mouth to make you shut up:

1 Paraphrase

2 Ask open questions

3 Debrief

Paraphrase

This is very simple and forces you to listen. When someone has said something and has reached a natural pause, it is tempting to pitch in with your own point of view. Avoid temptation. Instead, summarize in your own words what you heard the other person say. This does not signify agreement – it signifies only that you understood what they said and that you were listening. If you summarize wrong, they will correct you quickly and you will have avoided misunderstanding. If you summarize correctly, they will think that you are pretty smart because you have understood them. They will then feel emboldened to embellish what they have said. Paraphrasing builds understanding and respect. As a simple test, try paraphrasing what this section has said. As you paraphrase, you should also find it much easier to remember what has been said. If you say it, you remember it.

Ask open questions

This is a real art form. The right open questions will get the other person to focus and reflect on the right issues the right way. The key part of open questioning is to encourage the other person to give rich answers. The one thing to avoid is a closed question, which results in a yes/no-type answer.

Closed questions invite someone to take a position, which they then feel the need to defend. Avoid boxing them into a corner. Questions which fall into this trap often begin:

'Do you agree...'

'Shall we go to...'

'How much is...'

If you know you will get the 'right' answer to these questions, at the end of a discussion, they may be acceptable. If you get the 'wrong' answer, you will find yourself taking opposing positions and you are in a win/lose discussion.

Open questions invite rich answers. They avoid boxing people into a corner too early and allow options to be explored. As you let people talk, you let their trust in you build. Open questions often begin:

'Why did they…'

'What happened when…'

'How would you…'

Inevitably, letting people talk takes more time than simply telling them what to do. The lazy and heroic form of leadership is to tell everyone what to do. The longer and less heroic route is more productive. It teaches people to think for themselves, to own their own problems and to find their own solutions.

Debrief

If there were more than two of you at the meeting, always try to debrief around three questions:

▶ What did you hear/observe during the meeting?

▶ How were they reacting?

▶ Who does what next?

This need only take a few minutes. Inevitably, you will find that two people saw and heard different things. You will get far more value and intelligence out of the meeting by a quick debrief than by trying to take notes in the meeting. Note-taking simply gets in the way. It prevents observation. Writing obstructs thinking about how to manage the conversation. It puts the other people on their guard.

Learning how to write

Good business writing is one of those oxymorons which is up there with military intelligence, social services and head office help.* It is definitely a case of 'Do as I say, not do as I do'. None of us are likely to write as well as

---

* Try also: civil servant, controlled chaos, easy payments, collective responsibility, committee decision, job security, gourmet pizza, non-alcoholic beer, objective opinions and quick fixes.

our favourite novelist or screen writer. But at least we can save our colleagues from the kind of drivel that they impose on us from time to time.

For many years I was beaten up by an editor who kept on pulling my work apart. Eventually, I figured he caught me consistently on just five rules which I always broke, and still do too often.

1 Write for the reader.

2 Tell a story.

3 Keep it simple and short.

4 Make it positive in substance and in style.

5 Support assertions with facts.

This sounds easy. It is not; it requires real discipline and focus.

Write for the reader

Faced with the daily deluge of e-mail, you may occasionally wonder why you are wasting your time on so much trivia. Much of it was not meant for you. You have been copied on stuff on a just-in-case basis. But some e-mails have clearly been written for you personally. Even if they are poorly typed, with spelling errors and bad grammar, you are likely to read them. They are relevant to your needs and interests. The good writer thinks into the position of the reader and writes for that person. When this happens, clarity and focus are achieved. You can drop much of what you could write, and focus on what the other person needs to read. Avoid the trap of writing for yourself.

Tell a story

This does not have to be a literal story, like a nursery story or an adventure tale. Telling a story in business terms means marshalling the facts so that a coherent theme comes out with a beginning (here's the problem or opportunity) a middle (here's the detail) and an end (so what do we do next.) The story should pass the elevator test: you can summarize it to your boss in a fast moving elevator going a short distance. The virtue of telling a story is that it helps cut out all the noise that will confuse the message. Think of all the communications you receive every day: you really remember the headlines, not the detail. Focus first on getting the headline right, and then marshal the minimum required to back the headline up.

Keep it simple and short

Churchill wrote a long letter to his wife, Clementine, during the war. At the end he added a postscript: 'I am sorry I wrote you such a long letter: I did not have time to write you a short one.' Writing short is much harder than writing long. It requires real mental discipline. P&G used to be home of the one-page memo: young brand assistants had to summarize the entire progress of their brand for two months on to one page. It may have been single spaced with no margins, but everyone kept to the same discipline, which forces the writer to focus on what is important and does not confuse the reader with irrelevant detail. Another thing that helps the reader is to keep words and sentences short. Jargon, fancy words and complicated sentences impress the writer more than the reader.

Make it positive in substance and in style

People prefer to hear about opportunities and solutions rather than problems and difficulties. Be positive and sound positive. The classic bureaucratic trap is to write passively and in the third person: 'It has been ascertained that the following 27 points were deemed . . . to make your eyes glaze over with tedium.'

Support assertions with facts

The alert reader's shit detector will start squawking loudly when it encounters vague power words such as:

- ▶ important (to whom and why?)
- ▶ strategic (important with bells on)
- ▶ urgent (not to me, it isn't).

Avoid vague power words unless you can back them up. If it is important, show why. Supporting assertions with facts can also include using illustrations, examples and references to support your case. An unsupported assertion is always open to challenge.

Learning how to read

Words

We have a problem – you are reading this. So why on earth do you need to learn how to read when you are already reading?

There is a difference between reading for pleasure and reading for business. I hope you get some pleasure, even if you are not a masochist, from reading this. But I will assume that you are really reading this for business. You have my commiserations. By way of apology, let me tell you a story.

We were all sitting together in the old-fashioned partner's office. We all knew what all the other partners were doing; we did not need e-mail because we had ears. Most of the partners were very bright, but one of the partners, Bob, was about 100 watts short of brilliance. And yet the staff loved him and thought that he was brighter than the rest of us. This was deeply irritating to us.

One day I noticed Bob making some notes and I asked him what he was doing.

'I have some associates coming in. They are going to show me a draft of a document. I have not seen it yet. This is their little test to see if I am any use at giving feedback and to see if I am smart enough to understand their brilliant draft.'

I thought about this. I had always thought that associates bringing drafts was our chance to test them. Then I realized that Bob was right: they are also testing our ability as partners to add value to them. I asked Bob why he was making notes if he had not seen the draft in advance.

'Easy', said Bob. 'I always make a note of three things before seeing a document blind or listening to a presentation. First, I note my own view of the subject. I do not want to be swayed by their internal logic. The better their logic is, the more difficult it is to challenge unless you already have a clear point of view yourself. I do not read openly; I read with prejudice. It makes me a better critic.'

'Ouch', I thought. I always read openly, and I always found it difficult to rise above the brilliance of the internal logic presented to me. I asked him what else he was noting.

'Second, I note down all the topics I expect to see covered. This helps me spot those things which are hardest to spot – things which aren't there. It always surprises them when I see the invisible gaps.'

'And last?' I asked.

'I make a quick note of any coaching points I want to cover with them', replied Bob. 'It may be about writing style, analytic techniques, data presentation, whatever. They like it when I can give them something practical and positive to go away and work on.'

I suddenly realized that I had never learned how to read. I had read like an empty vessel waiting to be filled with other people's stuff. Socially, this is an enjoyable way of reading a novel. In managerial terms, it pays to read with prejudice and with an agenda:

- ▶ Know your point of view.
- ▶ Know what you expect to be covered.
- ▶ Have some coaching points ready.

Naturally, it is impossible to do this exercise for every e-mail you receive, and you probably do not want to spoil reading for pleasure with this discipline. But if the meeting, presentation or document is important, it pays to go in properly prepared.

Of course, you might discover other things as you review the document or listen to the presentation, but at least you are now reading or listening with focused intent. Naturally, those of you who already read with intent are probably wondering why this reading section is missing one critical element: the art of speed reading. This is because my prejudice is that it is better to read a little well than a lot poorly. And I cannot speed read. This disqualifies me from preaching about it.

Learning how to read: numbers

Managers use statistics the same way drunks use lamp posts – for support, not illumination. Numbers are armies of facts which can be marshalled in support of a business case. Numbers are rarely objective; they can all be spun and manipulated. Politicians know this better than anyone.

> **❝** *Managers use statistics the same way drunks use lamp posts – for support, not illumination.* **❞**

The numbers game finds its apotheosis in the spreadsheet. As managers we all know what answer we are meant to achieve in the bottom right-hand corner of the spreadsheet. The number might be an NPV in dollars, or a ROE/ROI percentage, or any other financial target. Knowing the answer we have to get to, we assiduously play the what-if game on the spreadsheet until, miraculously, the right answer appears.

Leaders learn how to read through these numbers. There are three golden rules for establishing the value of the numbers in front of you:

1 Know the person who created the numbers.

2 Know your business.

3 Test the assumptions.

Note what is missing from this list: numeracy, an ability to add numbers fast or any sort of mathematical brilliance. In the days before spreadsheets, being able to add fast helped; you could check whether columns added to the totals and often found discrepancies that way. In the world of the spreadsheet, the maths are likely to be sound. It is the thinking you need to worry about.

Know the person who created the numbers

A great proposal with wonderful numbers from an unknown person, or someone with a mediocre track record, has low value. A less impressive proposal from someone who has a great track record of delivering results is worth far more. If you are putting together some numbers or a proposal, it pays to have a credible leader on your team.

Know your business

Good leaders have a deep knowledge of their industry and their organization. They will know all the key numbers and ratios. Philip Green, the British retailer, can instantly recall how much of and at what prices he bought and sold different clothing lines. He can look at a clothes rack and guess accurately how much each item was bought for and its selling price.

You should not have to worry about whether the spreadsheet has calculated the numbers correctly. You should instead be able to spot an unlikely number and challenge it based on your business knowledge. I have often caught input errors, to the surprise of the staff who put them in, by simply questioning an unlikely looking ratio or number.

Test the assumptions

Spreadsheets have spurious accuracy and authority. We asked an actuary to project the profit on new product. The answer came back as a margin of 8.2873%, which was good. We then asked the actuary what would happen if interest rates rose or fell by 2%. Two days later the answers came back. The profit margin would rise to an extraordinary 33% (rounded) or fall to a catastrophic –25% (rounded). Spreadsheets do not provide the answer. They are a starting point for discussion. Used wisely, they will provide illumination rather than support.

Curiously, to read and challenge numbers well, there is no need to be numerate. Many numerate people lose themselves in the detail of the numbers. Less numerate leaders are at an advantage in interpreting numbers: they can step back and look at the person and the assumptions behind the numbers better and are more likely to challenge numbers which do not make business sense to them.

Learning how to meet

Meetings are a wonderful substitute for work or responsibility. They are also the essence of management. Try explaining what you do to a three-year-old. Saying that you are the Senior Executive Vice President for MegaCorp will simply see all the toys getting thrown out of the window. Explaining that you build CRM databases will not help much either. Whatever leaders do, in practice they spend most of the day meeting people. Even a three-year-old understands that, more or less.

So it pays to have effective meetings. Now think of what proportion of the meetings you have to attend are truly effective. You may be lucky, in which case move on to the next section. You may be like the majority of managers who find too much of a limited day being drained away in ineffective meetings.

**&& *Meetings, like Liquorice Allsorts, come in all shapes and sizes.* **

Meetings, like Liquorice Allsorts, come in all shapes and sizes. They range from informal one-to-one meetings to major conferences, from formal decision-making meetings of the board to brainstorming meetings of the staff. For the sake of brevity and sanity, this is not the time or place to explore every flavour of meeting. Effective meetings come down to three principles:

▶ right purpose
▶ right people
▶ right process.

Forests have been destroyed describing effective meeting processes. Let us save some trees and concentrate on the right people and the right purpose. If you have these, you are 80% of the way to success. If you do not have them, you are 100% of the way to failure.

The right people and the right purpose

After one particularly mind- and arse-numbing all-day meeting Dean, one of my mentors, looked very happy. I asked him what was wrong with him. He should have looked as unhappy as I felt. He explained he had three rules for any meeting. He applied them whether he was leading or attending the meeting, and it always helped him get a good result. Since then, the rules have been a productive guide for me to ensure that meetings have the right purpose and the right people:

▶ What do I want to learn?
▶ What will I contribute?
▶ What happens next?

Let's look at Dean's rules as applied to attending a meeting and leading a meeting.

Attending a meeting

Dean went to the all-day meeting with a very clear agenda, which had little to do with the official agenda. There were three people he had wanted to talk to, but they had all been elusive. He wanted to get some information and ideas from them. That was his learning rule. He also realized that the meeting gave him the chance to influence the CEO on one agenda item. He bade his time, and then moved in decisively on the one issue that mattered. Because he talked sparingly, when he did talk he commanded attention. He had fulfilled his contribution rule. By having both a clear learning and contribution objective, he had a series of follow-up actions with the CEO and the three people he had met. Everyone had left the meeting frustrated because nothing had been achieved in the formal agenda. Dean left happy because he had gone to the meeting with a clear intent and purpose, which he had achieved.

Leading a meeting

Dean applied his three meeting rules to meetings he chaired. He used the rules to decide who should attend. He expected each person to contribute something *and* to do something by way of follow up *and* to learn something useful. People could contribute by having decision-making power, having expertise or by having resources they could contribute.

Although the temptation to seek safety in numbers is great, it should be resisted. More people reduce effectiveness. Senior people want bag carriers to be present because they have the detail; bag carriers want to be there to get exposure to the senior managers. If the senior people cannot master the detail, they should not be there. They probably should not be senior managers.

The safety-in-numbers mentality is prevalent in the executive suite. The executive committee meets, but often the discussion dissolves into a series of bilateral discussions between the CEO and individual directors. Each director is a fully signed-up member of the mutual preservation society. The only rule of membership is that I will not piss on your turf if you do not piss on mine. So group discussion does not exist. Instead, each director plays a game of intellectual ping-pong with the CEO while the other directors are spectators waiting for their turn to have a game with the CEO.

Dean refused to let this happen. He would apply his three rules not just to the meeting as a whole, but to each agenda item individually. If an item was best handled bilaterally, he would not bring it to the larger group. This made his meetings small and effective. Also, everyone knew that the meetings were going to be effective and relevant to themselves, so they made a point of attending.

The right process

Having the right people and the right purpose for a meeting are essential. It also helps to have the right process.

There is a parlour game played on the radio called 'Just a Minute'. The object of the game is to speak for one minute on a chosen subject without hesitation, deviation or repetition. It is very difficult. The same principles should apply to the meeting process – to manage it without hesitation, deviation or repetition.

Hesitation is a product of starting late. It is nearly mandatory for senior people to turn up last or late. This shows that

▶ they are very busy

▶ their time is more important than yours, so you can wait.

They may be answering e-mails or practising the banjo, but they will still want you to wait. It is a common discourtesy that customers visit on suppliers, professionals on their clients, call-centre staff on their callers and managers on their staff. Live with it. Otherwise, putting up a clock in the office at least helps induce some guilt in those who are not shameless. As a leader you can set an example: be prompt and show that time is valuable and individuals are respected.

Hesitation also comes from a loose timetable. Time the meeting to be as short as possible to force the pace. The Privy Council meets standing up. This is a good way of keeping long-winded politicians short. It was particularly short when the late Queen Mother, aged 98, presided over the meeting. Sitting down is not mandatory.

There are some times never to hesitate. Never be disturbed by interruptions. Leaders should remain totally focused. I learned this in Manila during a period with many electricity outages. The first time it happened the room went pitch black. I hesitated: big error. Next time it happened, I carried on my presentation as if nothing had happened at all. The discussion flowed.

Deviation is a common cause of delay. People ramble off the subject or delve into minutiae. A good chairperson should not let this happen. If you set up the 'Just a Minute' rules at the start of the meeting, it becomes easy to challenge deviators; you can even keep score during the meeting. At minimum, make people give the headline before the text, as in a newspaper column. The headline tells people whether it is worth listening to or reading. It forces the speaker to think about what they want to say before they launch into a ramble.

Repetition normally happens when someone thinks they are not being heard properly. So they keep on coming back to the same point time and again, and again, and again. The rolling of eyeballs and looks of disbelief from everyone reinforces the repeater's belief that they are not being heard properly. Do not roll your eyeballs at repetition. Paraphrase the speaker to check you have heard what they are saying; this shows them that you are listening and they may shut up. If they raise the same point, repeat the paraphrase. Even the most obtuse participant should figure out that they have been heard and they are being repetitive.

The right process is helped by the right context. Dark, stuffy rooms do not help. The seating layout in the room does not have to be taken as given. I have become an expert furniture mover over many years of arranging meetings. How people sit affects the dynamics of the meeting. Having tea and coffee available is great, but the smell of hot food arriving at the back of the room loses an audience fast. Figure out the logistics that will make the meeting work for you and the attendees.

Learning how to communicate

The previous five sections have all been about communicating. But they have also been about something more subtle and more important – learning how to think and behave as a leader. The leader's mindset in communication has two main characteristics:

1 Being proactive

2 Decentring

Being proactive

For many people, reading and listening are naturally reactive processes. Being called to a meeting is a reactive event. Good leaders do not let themselves get led blindly by other people's agendas, words or presentations. They will proactively think of their own agenda, their own point of view. As a result, they will have a much more productive and insightful interaction with the person who thinks they are leading the meeting, presenting or writing the report.

Decentring

Effective leadership communication is not about clearly stating what you think. Good communication requires thinking your way into the head of the other person. If you can see the world through their eyes, you can start to communicate effectively with them. Your end goal remains the same; you still want to influence them. But the starting point is radically different. You start from where *they* are, not from where you are. Two journeys with the same destination will be completely different if they have different starting points.

❝ Good communication requires thinking your way into the head of the other person. ❞

Naturally, different people feel comfortable with different styles and forms of communication. Some like face-to-face communication; some prefer e-mail. Some play hard to catch behind a defensive secretarial wall. One leader is nearly impossible to contact. But send her a short text message and she will reply within an hour.

Great leaders do not have to be literary giants or brilliant orators. But all of them find ways of communicating clearly and effectively with all their stakeholders. Good communication requires focus, discipline and clarity. These are good disciplines for any leader to acquire.

PART THREE

Mastering leadership

8

Leading from the top

Strange things happen to people when they get to the top of an organization. They suddenly find that their jokes become funnier, their taste becomes impeccable and that their judgement becomes excellent. Everyone starts being nice to you. And everyone wants a slice of your time and a chunk of your support for whatever their interest is. Staff, suppliers and customers cluster around you like moths drawn to an artificial light at night.

This can be alarming. You make a casual suggestion to someone and suddenly find they are doing it: they have justified their idea on the basis that 'the boss says so . . .'. You come into the office and you are having a bad hair day. You find that your little personal cloud of gloom has spread like a major depression over the entire office.

This new-found power can go to people's heads. Until now they have had plenty of people competing with them for promotion and plenty of bosses to remind them, gently, when they are being daft. These disciplines disappear, because few people choose to challenge the CEO.

With the previous disciplines of competition and honest feedback disappearing, things can start to go wrong quickly. Typical traps include:

▶ Diving into the trough of status and entitlement. This is not just about becoming a greedy fat cat, despised within and beyond the organization. It is also about all the small signs of not caring: not sharing the pain of cost-cutting, retreating to the comfort of the CEO's office and enjoying the status symbols of reserved parking, nights at the opera and golfing parties at the weekend.

▶ Underestimating your influence. Everyone picks up their cues from you in terms of behaviours and direction. Innocent comments can get blown out of all proportion. Role-modelling the values of the organization becomes a challenge of never letting your professional guard slip.

▶ Riding the momentum of the organization. Many CEOs become stewards and custodians of a legacy they have inherited. This is a recipe for a quiet life. Leaders need to create a legacy, not live off one. They need a clear vision and direction.

▶ Overestimating their own capabilities. Some leaders become dictators who enjoy command and control and try to decide everything. This is often portrayed as heroic and brilliant leadership. It is more likely to be highly ineffective leadership; no one person has a monopoly of wisdom. In a changing and complicated world, smart leaders know their limitations and build a team which complements their own strengths and weaknesses.

❝ Smart leaders know their limitations and build a team which complements their own strengths and weaknesses. ❞

At this point, it is worth reminding yourself what people truly value in a leader at the top of an organization:

▶ ability to motivate others (people focus)
▶ vision (positive focus)
▶ honesty and integrity (professionalism: values)
▶ decisiveness (professionalism: skills)
▶ ability to handle crises (professionalism: skills).

Take a moment to think honestly about how well you score on each of those criteria. The table below shows the percentage of our respondents who were satisfied with their senior leaders on each of these five criteria:

Ability to motivate others	37%
Vision	50%
Honesty and integrity	54%
Decisiveness	50%
Ability to handle crises	47%

Most of our respondents felt their leaders had self-confidence (72%). The self-confidence of leaders in themselves is not mirrored by their followers. There is a large perceived leadership gap. What people say to your face and what they think behind their faces are not always the same thing. You will be the last person to find out that people think you suck.

If you do not have a coach whispering in your ear, the danger is that the first piece of honest feedback will come from the chairman when he fires you. With the career expectancy of a FTSE-100 CEO now below five years, tolerance of sub-par performance is evaporating fast. Everyone who becomes a leader thinks that they will succeed – the evidence is that an increasing number fail.

We will look in this section at how leaders can deliver against the five leadership criteria that are most valued. Some of them, like honesty and integrity, look absurdly simple. As we talked to our leaders, it became clear that this is a high hurdle to jump. Other criteria, like vision, look daunting; we cannot all be visionaries. But here we found some reassuringly practical and simple things a leader can do to create and communicate a vision.

Each leader has their own way of succeeding and failing. There is no universal formula for success. But by focusing on these five criteria and following some simple and practical tools from other leaders, you can at least load the dice in your favour.

9

Focusing on people

Leaders and the people paradox

The old adage says that it is lonely at the top. Objectively, a leader is never-lonely. Casual observation of any leader's day will show that it is a never-ending procession of meetings. Some may be formal, many are informal. Leaders want to find out what is really going on. They trust people much more than paper. The carefully crafted written word is there to make a case, not to tell the truth. Talking to trusted people gives a chance to test ideas, see reactions and get slightly closer to reality.

John Kotter, the HBS professor, studied how top leaders really spend their time. On average, less than 25% of their time is spent alone: thinking, writing, reading or attached to e-mails. Many leaders spend less than 10% of their time alone. Face time with others is not just in formal meetings. A large amount of the leader's time is spent informally with a vast array of people covering a vast array of subjects. A ten-minute meeting might easily cover five topics.

All of this runs counter to the received wisdom that the leader should structure each day for greatest efficiency – tightly scheduled and well-planned meetings together with scheduled reflection and thinking time. Of the leaders I interviewed, the closest one of them came to having personal thinking time was on his bicycle to work and in the toilet. The mobile phone was invading both of those sacred spaces in the day.

If leaders spend so much time with people, how come they fancy they are lonely?

Lonely in a crowd: people as issues, not humans

It is possible to be lonely in a crowd. As a leader you suddenly discover that everyone wants a slice of you; they want a slice of your time, your energy, your power, your resources, your insight. Some bring problems to deal with. Some bring solutions for which they want approval and authority. Everyone wants something from you. For them, talking to you as the leader has high stakes. For the leader, a casual conversation becomes a rare beast. Many CEOs can be found apparently wasting time using humour or making small talk; they want to deal with people, not just issues all day.

66 The loneliness of the leader comes from the changed nature of relationships with the rest of the organization. 99

The loneliness of the leader comes from the changed nature of relationships with the rest of the organization. The leader is in danger of finding that people cease to be humans and increasingly become issues which they need to deal with. This creates pressure for the leader and opportunities for those around them.

To counter the pressure of dealing with issues attached to people all day, many leaders create a kitchen cabinet – a group of trusted staff and advisors who can help them see through the issues and the people effectively. One CEO recruits a graduate entrant in their mid-twenties as a PA. The graduate is on the fast track, is no threat and can be the eyes, ears and hands of the CEO as needed. Many have personal coaches who they use as sounding boards. Many have staff attached to their office. All of these people exist outside the formal line structure of the organization and give the leader a source of trusted people and impartial advice.

The leader alone: in search of a peer group

The leader is lonely for another reason: he or she has no peer group with whom to interact regularly. A salesperson frequently sees lots of other salespeople and has a sales manager who knows all about the sales job. At every level of the organization there tends to be a peer group that is facing similar challenges. It is possible to learn from their successes and failures. The leader has no one else to observe as a peer on a daily basis. They also have no one to tell them that they are messing up. The first thing they hear about it is likely to be when the chairman sits down to discuss the severance package. The leader's style may be great or it may be awful. There is no benchmark to observe and no impartial feedback to enable the leader to calibrate performance regularly.

It was striking that most of the leaders interviewed on video were very keen to see the results. This was not just vanity of wanting to see themselves on video. Most can have that as much as they want. They really wanted to see what their peer group thought and how they would have handled the situations we talked about. They wanted to reach out to their peer group in a meaningful way. The attraction of conferences such as the World Economic Forum is less about the speakers and more about the chance to meet a peer group.

Leadership and the pinnacle of people practice

At the top, some things change, some do not. Perspectives certainly change at the top of the mountain. You can see forever on a clear day. The people at the bottom of the mountain will see the trout in the stream, the cat in the garden and the flowers by the road. None of this will be visible to the leader gazing across the distant ridges into the future. Neither view is right or wrong.

Some things do not change. The people skills, acquired en route to the top, do not change. The skills previously covered remain important:

▶ coaching

▶ influencing

▶ giving feedback

▶ handling conflict

▶ motivating.

These skills remain unchanged. The way leaders deploy these skills remains unchanged. The hard ass remains a hard ass; the tree hugger remains a tree hugger. By the time leaders have reached the top they have acquired perhaps a 20-year track record which states to them categorically that what they do is what works. They will not change a winning formula because some smart ass book or consultant says that there is a better way. They may adjust at the margins, especially if something goes wrong. But their underlying style will remain the same.

You learn your style of people management on the way up, not at the top.

The good news is that as a leader, you will now be spared any more theory telling you that you have been coaching, influencing and motivating the wrong way for the last 20 years.

The bad news is that there is yet more to be learned. All the leaders I interviewed had the humility and self-confidence to say that they are still learning as leaders. There are always new situations and new opportunities.

There are three new people-based skills the leader typically has to acquire:

1   Creating the top leadership team.
2   Leading the top leadership team.
3   Working with the board.

We will look at each in turn.

Creating the top leadership team

It is a truism that great teams achieve great things. Marry a great team to a great strategy and anything is achievable. Money need never be the constraint; talent is the constraint. Before we offer any instant recipes for talent success, let's look at some of the typical traps that leaders fall into.

▶ *Too much self-confidence.* Self-styled heroic leaders want to do it all themselves. They trust no one else. By making decisions themselves or overriding their team they demoralize and weaken their team. This is a vicious circle where the weaker the team becomes, the more the heroic leader believes in taking personal control. Even if the heroic leader succeeds for a while, they leave behind a weakened organization with no effective succession in place.

▶ *Too little self-confidence*. Not all leaders have the self-confidence to know and admit their own weaknesses. Instead, they look for people like themselves to fill the leadership team. The result is an inbred, dysfunctional, unbalanced team of yes-men who feel very happy in the leadership club. There is nothing to balance the leader's weaknesses, and their strengths are echoed redundantly by the rest of the team.

▶ *Excess humility and power loss*. Some leaders let themselves get captured by the power barons that reside in any organization. The barons make themselves indispensable. Dangerous power barons are budding heroic leaders. They take complete control of their part of the business and deliver results; it becomes impossible to see past them or manage through them. In investment banks, the barons threaten to take their teams across the road to a rival.

▶ *Excessive reason*. Some leaders fall in love with the logical side of business. They start to believe in drawing up organization charts with lots of boxes and putting people in the boxes. You should only put people in boxes when they are dead. Especially at the top, you need to deal with people, not boxes.

If we can turn these negatives around into positives, we find that the effective leadership team is based on four principles:

1 Balance
2 Power
3 Purpose
4 Shape

Balance

All the leaders interviewed had the self-confidence and self-knowledge to know their weaknesses. This is the first step in creating a balanced leadership team. Some of the weaknesses are obvious. Non-financial leaders need good financial support. Great strategic leaders need great operators at their side, as much as the great operator needs a great strategist nearby. Balance is also needed in style – a team of yes-men is as destructive as a team of prima donnas.

This sounds obvious, but it is not. The temptation for a leader is to design the ideal organization and then create the team to fit the design. Intuitively, many effective CEOs do it the other way round: they start with the people and then shape the organization to the team. It is better to have a slightly messy structure than a slightly dysfunctional leadership team.

> ❝ It is better to have a slightly messy structure
> than a slightly dysfunctional leadership team. ❞

Power

John Major, the British Prime Minister, was famously attacked by one of his colleagues, Geoffrey Howe, for 'being in office, not in power'. Major did not survive much longer in office either.

Just because leaders have titles, it does not mean they have power as well. Power needs to be acquired and used.

One of the easiest ways to seize power from the power barons is to reorganize. This has nothing to do with the logic of improving the structure or strategy of the organization. It is about making sure that the leader's power is recognized and respected. Move some power barons away from their fiefdoms so that they become dependent on you, not vice versa. If you lose a power baron or two, the rest will be cowed. Ritual executions have always exerted a strong fascination on the mob.

The dark side to reorganizing is obvious. There is also a more positive side. A reorganization is a chance to reset the psychological contract with each member of the leadership team. Working with one CEO on a reorganization, we designed all the predictable stuff about job descriptions, titles, roles, responsibilities and goals for each member of his leadership team. By far the most important part of the discussion was what the new psychological contract should be: working styles, mutual expectations and needs, risks and opportunities. This was the first step to creating a functioning team that existed in reality, not just on paper.

Purpose

A team without a purpose is as useless as a leader without followers. The effective leader needs to craft an agenda which is greater than the sum of the parts of the leadership team. There needs to be a *shared* purpose. The purpose of the team will help inform the required balance of the team; globalizing businesses need global capabilities.

Leadership vision is dealt with at length in Chapter 10. From the people perspective, it is the vision or purpose that transforms a collection of talented individuals into a leadership team pulling in the same direction.

Shape

Architects, at least those who exist in the pre-postmodern world, have always held that 'form follows function': the design of a building should reflect its purpose. What works for architects does not work for leadership.

For leaders, the motto should be 'people perform purpose'. In other words, figure out the purpose and the vision then assemble the right mix of skills and styles to achieve that purpose. The structure, or form, of the organization follows from the people and the purpose; it does not precede it. Putting people first annoys consultants who want neat and tidy organization charts. That is why you are the leader and they are not.

> **❝ The structure, or form, of the organization follows it from the people and the purpose; does not precede it. ❞**

Leading the top leadership team

Achieving clarity, focus and alignment

It is not easy to lead leaders. Exert too little control and they become power barons. Exert too much power and you become a caricature of the heroic leader, demoralizing and disempowering your team. Whatever your personal style may be, it will not suddenly change once you arrive at the top. As a leader, you will still find yourself inundated with managerial tasks such as monitoring performance. All the numbers have three or four more noughts on the end, but the basic task remains the same.

> **❝ It is not easy to lead leaders. ❞**

As a leader you need to decide where you are able to make a difference and add value to the team. In essence, there are three things that the leader of leaders can deliver:

1 Clarity

2 Focus

3 Alignment

Clarity

Clarity is not about the answer. Plenty of experts claim to know the answer. For the leader, the real challenge is to know the problem. In any organization, there are myriad challenges and opportunities. But there are limited resources and only 24 hours in the day. The effective leader has to cut through the fog of competitive and internal war, and cut through the deluge of daily detail to see the few opportunities and challenges that make the difference.

Focus

I have yet to meet a leader who wants less focus. Once you have clarity about the problem, then it should be possible to focus the organization on two or three must-win battles. If you have four must-win battles, the chances are that people cannot focus on them all. They will pick and choose and one or two must-win battles will be lost.

Alignment

Most leaders I interview have great clarity and focus. They talk passionately about exactly what they must achieve. There is just one problem with this. Different leaders in the same organization often have clarity, focus and passion around completely different things. They can be pulling energetically in different directions.

Achieving alignment is not just about strategy papers and aligning reward and measurement systems, although these are important. More important is creating a common vision. This is best done through the much derided off-site meeting. Away from the all-consuming trivia of daily management, the leadership team needs time to reflect and achieve common clarity, focus and alignment. If the vision is visual, a map of the future, so much the better: it avoids details, focuses on what is important and is more memorable than a long and worthy set of words.

The art of unreasonable management

Achieving clarity, focus and alignment sounds reasonable and rational. Effective leaders learn to be selectively unreasonable.

All leaders know the world is not getting any easier. Suppliers do not cut prices voluntarily, staff want more money and fewer hours, competition does not go to sleep and there are always regulators and tax officers who want another slice of your action. The result is that the performance baseline for an organization is not a steady state – it is faster or slower decline. All the profit improvement programmes promise more profit; in practice, they only keep the organization from decline.

The reasonable leader understands these constraints. There are always good reasons why targets may be difficult to hit. One electronics company was heading to bankruptcy. The president ordered a 20% cut in working capital and in head count, across the board. Each division head had an excuse:

'We just cut 20% from costs last year; we can't do it again.'

'Our benchmark costs are already best in class; you can't beat that.'

'You can't cut a business which is growing.'

The reasonable leader would have accepted these excuses, and the company would now be bankrupt. The unreasonable response was to insist on the 20% cut, and if it wasn't achieved, the division heads would become part of the 20%. Occasionally, the leader has to be unreasonable.

The art of unreasonable management is not confined to crises. Anyone who was sane would have told Fred Smith that his idea for FedEx, a nationwide overnight delivery service, was insane. Legend has it that he got a 'C' grade from his tutor at business school for the idea. Branson and O'Leary were nuts to take on British Airways. Soichira Honda was clearly deranged to think he could take on the might of the Big Three US auto manufacturers. Reasonable people do not create great empires. We all remember Alexander the Great. Who has ever heard of his uncle, Alexander the Reasonable?

There is a fine line between unreasonable and intolerable. The unreasonable leader will stretch the team; the intolerable leader will break the team. To make the goal more realistic, the leader will stage the challenge into stretching, but achievable, targets. Do not ask everyone to score a hole in one every time. Let them take as many shots as they need to get to the target. The important thing is to get to the target. Tackle it in bite-sized chunks, give support, be flexible about the means. But do not bend on the goal.

Working with the board

Much effort has been expended by worthy people on the subject of corporate governance. Most of the argument centres around finding the balance between achieving independence and providing relevant expertise on the board. Relevant experts are normally industry insiders, who will naturally be company insiders rather than competitors. So they are not very independent. Independent directors should, in theory, represent the interests of the shareholders effectively and control the executive. But they probably lack the in-depth expertise to challenge and monitor the executive effectively. It is easy to say that you need a balance between the two. If you are writing a report for the government on the subject, you have to write a little more detail than that. For leaders, this makes for a conversation if there is nothing better to talk about. In practice, leaders need to focus on what works, not on the theory of governance.

Operationally, the CEO needs to work out how to manage the board. In theory the chairman should do this. But a good CEO will have many years of experience of managing upwards. The same tools and techniques still apply at this exalted level.

- ▶ Avoid surprises: pre-warn, pre-wire, prepare the ground in advance.
- ▶ Agree expectations about working styles, roles and goals.
- ▶ Involve appropriately.
- ▶ Never bullshit or shade the truth.
- ▶ Deliver results.

Often, the trickiest relationship is between the CEO and the chairman. It is the chairman who hires the CEO and fires the CEO. There is, rightly, some tension in a good relationship here.

Part of the problem is that the CEO and the chairman often want to do each other's roles. The chairman, especially if they have been kicked upstairs from the CEO role, finds it difficult to let go. The chairman suffers the 'leader in the locker room' problem that first-time managers suffer. They want to play the game. This means they interfere too much and get in the way of the CEO.

In contrast, the CEO can get delusions of grandeur. It can be very appealing to be the spokesperson for the organization – talking to the media, romancing the financial analysts, and joining the ranks of the good and the great by becoming committee and commission person. Some of these things the CEO can do. Leave the rest to the chairman to keep them happily occupied and out of harm's way.

The real problem for the chairman is that they cannot see into the organization. Financial results are a lagging indicator of performance. By the time the financial results head south, it is too late to do much. CEOs, as Kotter discovered in his study, spend a disproportionate amount of time walking the corridors and finding out what is really going on. This is not a luxury that the board is allowed. They do not have the time, and they would get in everyone's way if they acted as an alternative leadership team.

In practice, the relationship will work where there are the following:

1 Performance
2 Clear expectations
3 Trust, stories, quick wins and no errors

Performance

The power of the CEO is directly related to performance. The better the performance, the more the board will feel unable to question or challenge the CEO. With the career expectancy of FTSE-100 CEOs falling below five years, there is a strong indication that CEOs are not performing to expectations and that boards are prepared to use their muscle.

The key word here is *expectations*. Managing both board and investor expectations is an essential art form.

Clear expectations

Any CEO knows about managing expectations from the earliest days of their management careers. They know that if you set the baseline as low as possible, it is easy to show you are making progress. If you accept the lunatic growth and profit projections you have inherited, you will be set up to lose.

It is no surprise that when a new CEO is appointed, there is a fairly predictable clearing out of skeletons from cupboards. The resulting write-offs set a low financial baseline and give some possibility of later write-backs.

Trust, stories, quick wins and no errors

Trust builds up over time, but many CEOs do not have time on their side. They need quick wins to show that they are in control and that they can be trusted. As much as anything else, the CEO needs to sell the board a story. You can call the story a strategy, to impress the board. But, in practice, it is normally a very simple story which even a non-executive board member can remember when being entertained at the opera. The stories which work are as simple as:

- ▶ We will focus on the basics (no strategy, just operational excellence).
- ▶ We will grow internationally.
- ▶ We will refocus on our core business (i.e. sell non-core assets).
- ▶ We will be number one or two in every market where we compete (e.g. GE).
- ▶ We will leverage our brand into similar markets.
- ▶ We will concentrate only on major, global brands (e.g. Unilever).

These simple stories may be built on deep strategic analysis and insight. This is where management consultants like McKinsey or Monitor are useful; board members want their stamp of approval. They outsource their thinking to consultants. But it all comes back to something simple.

Equally, the consequences of the story can be dramatic and give rise to early wins:

- ▶ Reorganize the top team.
- ▶ Sell a business or two.
- ▶ Drop an expensive project.
- ▶ Drop an underperforming product line.

These early wins help the CEO buy time. The non-executive can now go to the opera and recall that you not only Have A Plan, you are also Doing Something. They can now relax and watch the opera.

For the board, financial performance is their main indicator of how well the CEO is doing. But it is a lagging indicator of performance; once the results are in, there is nothing they can do about it. The only other evidence they have of performance is how you perform in board meetings. This means spending perhaps a disproportionate amount of time in engineering the board meetings for success – late, missing or faulty papers are corrosive of trust. Attention to detail may not be the CEO's strength, but it is the detail the board notices. Equally, the board likes to feel involved in the business; the CEO needs to throw them the right bones to chew on. Put practically, the more they are involved in crafting and approving your strategy, the harder it will be for them to distance themselves from it if it goes wrong.

The CEO finds that all the old disciplines of building trust and commitment, selling ideas, influencing people and building networks apply at board level as much as they ever did in the past. It is a case of back to the future for the CEO.

10

Being positive

All leaders inherit a position and a legacy in terms of an organization, strategy, resources and performance. This is good news and bad news. The legacy gives something to build on. But the legacy can also be a prison. Organizations assume a life and a momentum all of their own. It is easy to be trapped by the existing legacy and momentum. This is the low-risk option: if it ain't broke, don't fix it. If you do try to change things, you will find the inertia of the organization is against you. Neither organizations nor individuals enjoy change or risk.

Leaders who simply maintain the inherited legacy are more like stewards of a business and less like leaders. Stewardship is respectable. If you are the CEO of the Grosvenor Group, which is 350 years old, you have to have enough humility to recognize that your primary role is to be a great steward of the business. You do not need the arrogance of a leader who decides to change the old property business into a funky new-age dot.com bankruptcy.

The leader needs to navigate between the two extremes of being passive and being revolutionary. The leader needs a positive vision of where the organization is going and how it is going to get there, and the vision needs to be communicated positively.

Speed readers will have missed that. So to reinforce the point, the positive agenda for the leader has three elements:

1 Creating the vision.
2 Communicating the vision.
3 Enabling the vision to happen.

We will look at each of these elements below.

Creating the vision

The vision thing can be pretty daunting. It sounds like we have to be able to lead our people out of the desert and into the promised land.

I tried the vision thing once. I got as far as 'I have a dream…' and gave up. My last dream had been about a cloud of intergalactic flying teacups. This might have inspired some shrinks and amused the staff. But it would not have helped the organization achieve its goals.

Visions and visionaries can be dangerous. Mao, Pol Pot, Marx and Hitler all had visions which collectively killed hundreds of millions of people. Some visions take you to the promised land; others take you straight back into the desert.

**❝ Some visions take you to the promised land;
others take you straight back into the desert. ❞**

Despite this, the best leaders have visions, but they are not necessarily visionary. To their surprise, they find that they have always had visions. Their visions are very simple. Typically, they work because they show three things:

▶ Where we are going, and why that is relevant to each person. Increasing EPS is not very meaningful to the receptionist.

▶ How we will get there, and that getting there is possible.

▶ What the vision means to each person: it is communicated well.

This is pretty simple stuff. The simpler it is, the better. In today's world we suffer a surfeit of choice. The resulting complexity and confusion are impediments that we cannot afford. A good vision creates clarity and helps people at all levels make better decisions. The vision must be simple enough that it can be interpreted and made relevant for shareholders, trustees, staff, suppliers and customers.

Before looking at grand corporate visions, think about the visions you have already crafted. Anyone who has led a project team, even of two or three people, has probably crafted a vision for the team which meets the criteria above:

- ▶ Here is where our project is going and what we need to achieve; this is your role in helping us get there.
- ▶ Here is the workplan for how we will get from where we are to where we are going.
- ▶ You communicated the vision clearly and simply to the team.

Thought of like this, a vision becomes simple and natural. We do not need to announce that 'We will fight them on the beaches…'. All we need is a very clear articulation of where the organization is going. A message which is sophisticated and clever is useless. It will either not be understood at all or it will be misunderstood.

The need for a simple direction becomes more important as the world becomes more complicated and change happens at least as fast as ever. In practice, it takes either genius or courage to create simplicity out of complexity.

It's time to look at some effective visions in practice.

Good visions give everyone a very clear idea of where they are going, what they are meant to do and what they should not do. They can come in many shapes and many fashions. Here are four to get started:

1 NASA: 'to put a man on the moon and bring him back alive again'.
2 Lloyds Bank: shareholder value.
3 The Red Arrows: the perfect show.
4 Ryanair: the low-cost airline.

These are all mind numblingly simple and obvious statements. They do not take long to understand. They provide total focus on what is important. In each case the vision drives the organization.

NASA

When John F. Kennedy announced in 1962 that the United States would, before the end of the decade, put a man on the moon and bring him back again alive it was an outrageous statement. No one knew if this was possible. It was a compelling vision because the competition, the Soviet Union, had beaten the United States into space first with Sputnik and then with Yuri Gagarin.

The force of the vision was such that even setbacks such as losing astronauts on the launchpad in a Gemini disaster were seen as spurs to greater effort rather than vision ending crises. Ultimately, NASA succeeded.

Success was a curse from which NASA has never recovered. Outside NASA, few people know or even care what its mission is. It may not have a mission. It has no clear direction: it has some hits (Hubble) and some misses (Shuttle disasters). Where it goes next is anyone's guess.

Lloyds Bank

Brian Pitman, CEO and then chairman of Lloyds Bank, inherited a troubled bank which had branches scattered across all the parts of the globe that had once been coloured pink: the old British Empire. His vision was, at the time, revolutionary. Instead of building an empire, Lloyds would focus on building shareholder value. The implications were huge. Out went all the underperforming outposts of empire. In came a relentless focus on the domestic retail market, driving the cost–income ratio down through internal cost control and aggressive takeovers within the UK market.

For a while, Lloyds became the most valuable bank in the world. Then it hit the limit of UK market share the regulators would permit. Takeovers were no longer possible, and the vision was compromised. Like NASA, it suffered the curse of success and has arguably lost its pre-eminence in global value.

The Red Arrows

The Red Arrows are the air display team of the RAF. They have a clear vision – to achieve the perfect air show. They do not try to mark themselves against other air show teams. The only measure of success is perfection.

The search for perfection pervades everything they do, from careful selection of team members, planning of each mission and detailed debriefing of each mission afterwards to see what they need to do better to reach perfection. They have total clarity and focus on what is important to them.

Ryanair

There are many ways for airlines to compete: in-flight service, loyalty schemes, convenient schedules, route network, legroom, on-board entertainment, quality of food and wine, airport lounges, sleeper beds, punctuality, choice of airport, or quality of connections.

Michael O'Leary, the founder of Ryanair, has a simple response to all these competitive challenges: low cost, low cost, low cost, low cost, low cost, low cost, low cost, low cost, low cost, low cost.

This is very simple, very focused and very effective. Everyone, including the customer, understands what this means for them. Everything flows from the low-cost focus:

- ▶ Aircraft: one type to minimize costs.
- ▶ Marketing: cut out travel agent, minimize costs.
- ▶ Ticketing: electronic confirmation, no costly paper.
- ▶ Punctuality: high to maximize fleet usage, minimize costs.
- ▶ Airports: secondary airports, low landing fees, quick turnarounds.

As a low-cost carrier, they have a different market and different model from the flag carriers and are best positioned to survive the shake-out of the low-cost carrier market. In contrast, the staff of flag carriers find themselves confused by serving different markets (budget travellers and premium business travellers) with different messages and different needs. The difference is visible to all: on British Airways you see businesspeople in suits. A suit is rare on Ryanair.

An effective vision has several key elements:

▶ It helps focus the organization on the few must-win battles for the future.

▶ It helps focus people on what they should not do.

▶ You could not (easily) substitute the name of any other organization into the vision; it is unique to the strengths and aspirations of the one organization.

▶ The vision can be made relevant to different stakeholders from shareholders to new front-line workers.

▶ It is short, simple and everyone can remember it.

The four visions above meet these criteria reasonably well. Test the vision of your organization against these criteria.

Communicating the vision

CEOs like to read the company newsletter and annual report. There are normally lots of flattering photographs of the CEO looking magisterial behind a desk, looking dynamic at a company site, looking important with a royal or a government minister and looking generous and sociable at a company awards event. Generally, the role of company newsletters is to confirm to the CEO that they are a wonderful person.

Now think back to when you started work. How often did you read the company newsletter or believe what it said? Sadly, some CEOs still think that a few elegantly written articles, a couple of inspirational e-mails and a lavishly produced video supported by an equal lavish company conference will build excitement and commitment to the new vision. Think again.

Staff and other stakeholders have other things to think about besides your vision, like mortgages, shopping, holidays, bills and the weekend. Your vision probably comes somewhere below buying the cat food. The cat will survive without your vision but will not survive without some food. It takes real effort to make people take notice, let alone take action, as a result of your vision.

Communicating the vision is a combination of broadband (one-to-many) communication and narrowband (one-to-one) communication.

Communicating the vision in broadband

Successful communication comes down to three elements:

- one consistent message
- constant repetition
- multiple methods of communicating.

Look back to the successful visions. They could be summarized in one sentence or just a phrase. If you have a clever and complicated vision, throw it out. Make it simple and you have a chance of its being remembered.

Constant repetition gets the message home.
Constant repetition gets the message home.
Constant repetition gets the message home.
Constant repetition gets the message home.
Constant repetition gets the message home.
Constant repetition gets the message home.
Constant repetition gets the message home.
Constant repetition gets the message home.
Constant repetition gets the message home.
Constant repetition gets the message home.

Do not try to be subtle. I will confess to being guilty of creating some Daz advertising. Over 40 years the basic message has not changed: Daz is great for whiteness. It is not subtle, but at least people seem to remember the basic message. Even if you have repeated the message many times to the same group, do not assume that you can move on to other messages. Repeat it again.

Finally, use multiple methods of communication. Some are obvious – newsletters, e-mails, company conferences, meetings, training events, the website and walkabouts all give the chance to hammer home the message. The more you talk about it, the more challenge and feedback you will receive and the better you will become at communicating the message and refining it for each audience.

Multiple methods of communication are not just about the medium used (newsletters versus e-mail). They are also about finding creative ways of expressing the message. Here are some examples of how to be creative without looking like the spaced-out members of your advertising agency's creative team:

▶ SAS under Jan Carlsson decided to focus on the business traveller who required high service. 'High service' is important but vague as an idea. So he developed the idea of 'the moment of truth': every interaction with a customer is a moment of truth where you either build satisfaction and loyalty or you lose it.

▶ FedEx delivers parcels and documents overnight and on time. This is pretty clear, but it lacks drama. So Fred Smith created the idea of the 'Golden Package'. Any one package could be the golden package which transforms a client business or brings happiness to a family. Suddenly, the need to deliver every package on time despite any disasters en route became clear to every employee.

Celebrate successes and war stories. When you find someone who has done something that embodies the vision you are creating, recognize them and reward them in public.

Communicating the vision in narrowband

Ultimately, leadership is an engagement sport. You cannot lead by remote control. As John Le Carré wrote: 'A desk is a very dangerous place from which to view the world.' This is as true of leaders as it is of spies.

The leader needs to create a team and a network of people who have faith in the vision. Clearly, the leader's top team need to buy in. If they do not buy in, they need to move on. A team which is playing against itself is unlikely to succeed.

Less obviously, the leader needs to engage a specific network of individuals across the organization. You need to get the informal grapevine of the organization working for you. Relying on broadband media to get your message across is not enough. Newsletters tend to have the style and credibility of *Pravda* in the days of the Soviet Union. You need to get up close and personal with the owners of the grapevine.

Some of this will happen in the natural, semi-random process of meeting different people in different situations. In practice, there are a few individuals who are likely to carry informal influence out of all proportion to their formal position in the organization. They might run a social club. They might be the crusty old-timer who has seen it all many times before and has seen CEOs come and go with regularity. These people can spread poison, but they can also spread hope. Because they are outside the formal hierarchy they are trusted, and because they have wide networks they are influential. These are the people who feed the grapevine; if they say the new vision makes sense to them, people listen.

One chief executive reviewed the first three years of his tenure and estimated that over half of his time was spent on communicating the vision. People do not get it easily. You have to be creative about how you communicate.

John Timpson owns and runs a chain of 650 shoe repair shops. This is potentially one of the dullest, smallest and most dead-end industries that anyone could inflict on themselves. But he has made his business a success, and his employees are proud to be part of his firm. To succeed, he realized that he was as much in the customer service business as the shoe repair business. Good service meant more custom. He also realized that it was easier to hire good people and train them to repair shoes than to hire grumpy cobblers and train them to be happy and service-focused staff. He realized he needed a revolution.

Timpson trained his area managers to select staff on service aptitude, not technical skills. They listened and they did not get it. They still hired cobblers, although they now avoided the grumpiest cobblers. They hired slightly grumpy cobblers.

Eventually, Timpson changed the hiring assessment form. All the words went out. In came pictures of 'Mr Men'. Mr Neat, Mr Happy, Mr Prompt, Mr Smart and Mr Reliable all were on one side of the form. Mr Messy, Mr Late, Mr Dirty and Mr Lazy pictures were on the other side of the form. The area managers had to circle which of the Mr Men each recruit most resembled. The area managers got it, and the staff revolution began. Timpson's pulled away from all the traditional cobblers with great service from great staff who kept the customers happy and loyal.

Enabling the vision to happen

There are many people with lots of great ideas. And you will never lack for advice. Everyone will have a view on what you should do and where you are messing up. If you want ideas, read the newspapers. From the features pages to the horoscopes there are endless ideas about what people should do.

The hallmark of the leader is the ability to make things happen. Virtual visions are daydreams. They need to move from virtual reality to reality.

❝ Virtual visions are daydreams. They need to move from virtual reality to reality. ❞

Enabling the vision to happen is not easy. Prime ministers come with great hopes of what they will do once in power. But even prime ministers find it difficult truly to change society the way they want. As a test, think back for as many prime ministers as you can, and think what they are remembered for. Few of them are likely to leave much more than one major legacy to history. Sometimes, like Chamberlain's famous piece of paper from Munich, it is not the legacy they hoped for. Now do the same test for your own organization. If you can remember any of the previous CEOs, what was their major legacy? How will your successors remember you, if at all?

In reality, both nations and organizations assume lives of their own. No one person controls the whole organization. No one can know exactly what is happening everywhere all the time, let alone change it all. There are a limited number of things that the CEO can, in practice, control. The CEO has more levers of power than anyone else in the organization. But, unlike the Pope, the CEO is not infallible. Unlike God, the CEO is neither omnipotent nor omnipresent. Most, but not all, CEOs know this.

In practice, the leader has five generic levers of power that most leaders in most organizations use most of the time. Most leaders choose to exercise direct control over a few activities which are central to the success of the organization. The levers of power determine *how* the change can be enabled. The activities the leader controls directly determine *what* the leader will change. Everything else has to be delegated.

The five generic sources of power for the CEO are:

1 Strategy
2 Resource allocation and management
3 Reward and measurement systems
4 People: team formation
5 Structure

All five power levers are closely connected. The degree of change a leader achieves is reflected in how far each of these levers of power are pulled. Leaders do not have to be revolutionaries. Companies such as P&G do not survive by going through constant revolution. For decades P&G held the humbler, evolutionary, vision of doubling in size every ten years. That calls for 7% real growth every year. Double in size every ten years, and after 150 years you will be 32,000 times bigger than today. That is a lot of detergents and personal-care products for the world.

Strategy

This flows directly from the vision of the CEO. There is a nice philosophical debate about the difference between a vision, the mission, a strategy, goals and objectives. Get it wrong and your business school professor may have you burned at the stake for heresy. Risking the *auto de fe*, we will assume that strategy provides the framework for realizing the vision. The vision shows where we are and where we will go. The strategy shows how we will get there. It provides the framework for setting appropriate goals, allocating resources and priorities and going to market the right way.

A good strategy helps the organization focus in the right areas and make the right trade-offs in all the ambiguous decisions that departments face. It will help people decide what not to do, as well as what they should do.

Resource allocation and management

This is one of the two major ways in which the strategy finds expression in the organization. For good reasons, the annual budget cycle in most organizations follows close on the heels of the strategy review. The strategy review sets the framework and the priorities; the budget review makes the priorities real.

It is in the resource allocation process that the leader learns to be unreasonable. There are always reasonable reasons for budgets to be increased as salaries and supplier costs increase. Turning a deaf ear to reason and turning on the pressure is standard operating practice in this cycle.

Resource management represents much of the weekly and monthly grind of management and leadership. Budget variances are rarely positive; dealing with the consequences of negative variances is time consuming but critical.

Leaders rarely rely on just the formal resource management systems. Reports and spreadsheets give a version of the truth, and it is often the version that the reporter wishes to present rather than the one the leader needs to hear. Spreadsheets ensure that the maths are right. They do nothing for the logic or assumptions. Leaders compensate for the deficiencies in the formal reporting systems in two ways:

▶ They develop an intimate knowledge of the key numbers. This has inelegantly been styled as tuning a very sensitive shit detector. The leader knows the numbers and trends well enough that an odd number looks, well . . . odd. It merits further investigation by the shit detector.

▶ Leaders wander around the organization, talking to people at all levels and in all areas. They want to get behind the numbers and the formal reports. They have an insatiable appetite, or paranoia, to find out what is really happening in their organization.

Reward and measurement systems

These are the second way in which strategy finds expression in the organization. They frequently go wrong. The two major problems are:

▶ setting the wrong incentives

▶ misaligning incentives.

Wrong incentives abound. In several banks, loan officers are still rewarded on the size of their book, not on loan quality. In good times, this is not too important. As the tides of recession flow in, be prepared for the routine hand wringing of bank CEOs as they write off billions of dollars of bad debt. Inevitably, they will blame the economy, not their own lending and reward systems. Lending money is easy; getting it back is hard.

Misaligning incentives is an even more common problem because it is genuinely difficult to achieve. It is natural that sales, IT, operations and HR should have different objectives. This leads to different priorities and to conflict where neither side is objectively right or wrong. They both have goals to defend. In theory, it should be possible to design goals which are perfectly aligned across the organization. In theory, anyone can win the lottery if they enter. In practice, it is through the process of conflict and disagreement that the priorities of the organization are effectively established. Where there is conflict between groups, it pays not to listen too closely to the rational arguments. Look instead at how each group is being measured and rewarded. They are going to be eloquent and rational in defending what may be irrational goals. Changing the goals and measures is often the best way of cutting through irreconcilable differences between departments.

> ❝ *In practice, it is through the process of conflict and disagreement that the priorities of the organization are effectively established.* ❞

People: team formation

The partners of a consulting firm did a test at their summer retreat. Each partner led a team on one common problem that the Brazilian office faced. No one knew the details, other than those written up for the case. There were five teams. Five different answers came back, suggesting the client should:

- ▶ cut costs
- ▶ merge with another company (be acquired)
- ▶ acquire another company
- ▶ open new distribution channels
- ▶ restructure the top team.

Each answer reflected the strengths and interests of the partner concerned: the cost-cutting partner suggested cost cutting; the marketing partner suggested the new distribution channels.

The answer was not a result of the problem, it was the result of the person looking at the problem. There are several potential lessons from this, such as be careful of consultants and of unfamiliar Brazilian organizations. The most important lesson is that the strategy you get for the organization will be a function of the top team you put in place. You will not get great market-led growth from a restructuring and cost-cutting team.

No leader can control a large organization single-handedly. Leadership is a team sport. The hallmark of good leaders is that they create good teams around them to push their vision and strategy into the organization. As we have seen, *good* is not an absolute term. Good is about fit, not perfection. An organization in crisis may well need a team of experienced cost cutters; an organization intent on rapid growth may seek to make their leadership team more professional and introduce more disciplined market-focused capabilities.

Structure

Restructuring is a favourite of management. It is easy to do – shuffle the boxes around on pieces of paper. It is highly visible. It shows that you are doing something. In practice, there are two forms of restructuring, with quite different motives and impact.

Restructuring the top team

This is essentially a political act which new leaders often undertake. It is a way of exerting power over the organization: removing power barons who need to be removed, and opening up positions for the sorts of people that the new leader wants in the team. In other words, the restructuring is more about people than it is about structures. This makes the restructuring no less valid, except in the eyes of middle managers. They have seen it all before: the carousel goes round. Centralization and decentralization; shifting the matrix from geography to clients to functions and back again. What goes round, comes round. Rarely does restructuring itself transform the prospects of the organization, however much hot air is expended in selling the relative merits of one structure over another. But restructuring as a vehicle for putting the right leadership in place is essential.

Restructuring the business

This is, again, highly visible and shows the leader is doing something. It is loved by investment bankers (fees), consultants (fees), lawyers (fees), accountants (fees) and PR people (fees). Once they have helped you build an empire and saddled you with debt, they will help your successor dismantle the empire, collecting their fees a second time around.

Restructuring the business can have a dramatic effect on the fortunes of the business, for better or for worse. In each case, the challenge is to make sure the restructuring is driven by the strategy, not by the advisors. Research shows that acquisitions destroy value for shareholders in about 80% of cases; all the value is transferred to the shareholders of the acquired organization. This misses the political reality of acquisitions: the acquiror gets to play with a bigger toy. The acquired has lost the game.

❝ The political reality of acquisitions: the acquiror gets to play with a bigger toy. ❞

Crafting a leadership agenda

Besides these generic levers of power, each leader will normally choose two or three initiatives which they will control personally. These will reflect the main priorities of the organization. In many organizations this will be some form of change programme. But some leaders look for much greater focus, for instance:

1 The insurance company (brand, technology, people)
2 The systems house (deal making)
3 The consulting company (key clients and IP)
4 The non-profit (external constituencies)
5 The bank (people, systems, property)

The insurance company

Insurance is a technical industry; actuaries make rocket science look simple. For many years, the industry was led by actuaries. As a result, the industry became a museum of management malpractice – high costs, internal focus, customers coming last, and opaque profits and reporting. As life insurance clients signed up for 25-year contracts, there was not much pressure to perform. So the way was open for new insurance companies to come in. They did not need to be excellent to win. They needed to be less incompetent than the incumbents. Direct insurers such as Allied Dunbar (life insurance) and Direct Line (general insurance) started to take real market share away from the incumbents.

The incumbents had to enter the world of twentieth-century management fast. One leader came in to turn around an ailing incumbent and focused on just three items:

▶ brand
▶ technology
▶ people.

There was nothing about actuarial work, complex product development and all the traditional concerns of insurers. This was about efficiency, effectiveness and market presence. Branding was a new language to the company. It was not a matter of putting a few marketing types into an obscure office; it was about changing the locus of power from actuaries to the market place. This clearly required new people, new skills and new processes. The technology need was driven by the desire to lower costs and improve customer focus dramatically. It resulted in redesigning processes to support the new brand and service orientation.

Within such a revolution there are countless challenges. The leader realized he only had 24 hours in a day: he picked the battles where he could have the biggest impact and delegated as much of everything else as possible.

The systems house

Systems companies do things like integrating systems and outsourcing the technical infrastructure of an organization. So it is natural to think that leaders should perhaps support the occasional client mega-deal and be technically focused.

One leader realized that this was not where he could add most value. He did not focus on clients or on technology; he focused on deals. He realized that there were many sub-scale systems houses doing good work. But they could only serve small, local or regional clients. These clients could not or would not pay top dollar. Billing rates were about half what the major players like IBM or EDS charged. By pulling the smaller systems houses into a large international network, he gave them brand power and pricing power, while he got access to skills and technology.

So the CEO went shopping. He gained a black belt in shopping for systems houses and then integrating them into the network. He built a deal team which always negotiated well on price. It was a winning focus: buy a company which is charging out its staff at $100 an hour, and raise billing rates over three years to $150 an hour, which is still cheaper than the $200 an hour being charged by competition.

This is a strategy which has been replicated with varying degrees of success by both accounting and legal firms. The degree of success is directly related to the capability and focus of the leader in deal making and management. The leader does not need to be a professional lawyer, technologist or accountant. The leader needs to focus on those activities where they can best add value to the rest of the organization.

The consulting company

If you are ever given the chance to run a consulting company, don't. It is full of prima donnas who are good and they know it. They are not keen on being managed. They know exactly how much economic value they have added to the partnership and are keen to extract at least that much value back again. No leader in the industry can escape the grind of herding the cats at the top of the organization. It goes with the territory. But an effective leader needs more.

Most leaders in most professional firms enjoy their profession too much to want to go into management roles. They want to lead by example. One leader did so explicitly. He decided to build the global presence outside the United States by doing it himself. So he left the security of an established office and clients in the United States, bought a plane ticket to Europe and set up shop. His partners bade him 'adieu', not 'au revoir': they did not really expect to see him back again.

He focused on three things:

- ▶ Key clients. He took personal responsibility for acquiring and serving key clients. No clients, no revenues, no office. A key client at the start was anyone who would pay for a meal. It soon became anyone who would pay over $100k, then $500k, then $1 million and beyond.

- ▶ Hiring great staff. He hired ahead of the demand curve, which is dangerous. He was building costs without revenues. He figured that if you attract and retain great people, they will attract and retain great clients.

- ▶ Intellectual property. The defining difference of the company was its network of business school faculties that helped keep clients at the leading edge of management thinking and practice. He built this network outside the United States.

Within five years, the international business was larger than the American business he had left behind.

The non-profit

Non-profit management is at least as demanding as for-profit management. The non-profit does everything the for-profit does, but without the resources. It cannot spend its way out of trouble. It has to use creativity and capability, not cash. Except for the best endowed non-profits, the non-profit always lives on the edge of triumph and disaster. Fire fighting is standard operating practice. The normal operating mode for the CEO is to be manning the pumps at the fire hydrant. This is a familiar experience even with for-profit CEOs. But it does not make progress for the organization.

Ultimately, the distinctive contribution of one CEO came through managing the external constituencies of the organization. Creating the network of financial supporters, contributors in kind, political support and service delivery support created the framework and the stability for the organization to survive and thrive. Key staff might pave the way in developing and running the relationships with the external constituencies; having top cover from the CEO in securing the relationship at a senior level with the external partner was essential to success.

The bank

All banks worry about balance sheet management – acquiring deposits and making loans and (hopefully) getting the loans back at some point. They tend to have a lot of people who are very good at these activities. So the question for the leader is where should they focus their efforts? Most leaders of banks have deep expertise in balance sheet management. That, arguably, is the last place they should focus their discretionary effort. Other people can do that for them. One leader had to decide where he could add distinctive value.

He realized that the way to grow profits was to become the lowest-cost competitor in the market. Internal cost control was necessary, but not sufficient to achieve the goal. He also had many able people who could control costs. The way to lower costs significantly was through mergers. There were scale economies to be achieved which internal cost control alone could not deliver.

The scale economies came in three areas:

▶ Technology. You need one set of systems, not two, after merging. But it takes time and money to deliver these savings.

▶ People. People are expensive and you do not need so many of them after a merger.

▶ Property. Most banks are by default property companies. They own large chunks of the high street. After the merger, there is no point in owning two banks with different labels next to each other. One gets sold off to become a coffee shop or wine bar.

None of these three activities is a traditional banking activity, but all were critical to the vision of becoming the lowest-cost competitor. The leader was focusing on where he could add value and was delegating more traditional banking activities to the many able bankers within his organization.

There are two common features in each of these cases. They have implications for all leaders. The leaders in each case focused on activities which:

▶ Supported the distinctive vision of the company. They did not represent business as usual.

▶ Represented a way of the leader adding value to the organization. They were not doing things which other people could do.

Ultimately, leaders have to create their own role. This freedom can be unnerving. It is tempting to do what you have done before, but on a larger scale. This probably means that you are simply replicating some skills set which is already abundant in the organization. If other people can do something as well as you can, let them do it. If you do the same as them, you add no value.

Freedom gives the leader the ultimate challenge of showing where they can distinctively add value to the organization.

11

Being professional

It is a brave person who would dare to accuse a leader of being unprofessional. In extreme cases the brave person turns out to be the district attorney who accuses some leaders of various forms of kleptocracy.

Aside from the extreme cases, most leaders are professional. Professionalism takes many forms. The way in which the leader is professional is vital. It shapes the culture of the entire organization. In this chapter we will take a tour of four aspects of the professional leader:

1 The must-have personal and professional values.
2 Alternative styles of leadership.
3 Creating values for the organization at large.
4 Making the values real.

For leaders in the middle of the organization, professionalism focused mainly on core skills, especially communication skills. For leaders at the top, professionalism concerns the values and style of the leader and the organization.

The must-have personal and professional values

After interviewing the leadership group it became clear that there are as many different styles of leadership as there are leaders. Each leader has created a unique leadership DNA which works for them in their current situation. Copying the DNA is an exercise in futility; it is impossible to achieve and irrelevant. What works for one leader in one situation may not work for another in another situation.

In the interviews each leader talked about different values. Words like *courage, empathy, decisiveness, respect for the individual* and *determination* all cropped up. But only two words came up consistently, both from the leaders at the top of the organization and from people lower in the organization. Both words came as a surprise. The two key words were *honesty* and *humility*.

Honesty

The leaders' constant calls for honesty implied that they were less than happy with the levels of honesty they observed in other leaders. This implicit criticism was echoed explicitly by the followers who saw that there was insufficient honesty among their leaders. Only 54% of followers said that they were satisfied with the honesty of their leaders. This should be a wake-up call to leaders who tend to be self-confident individuals: 72% of followers thought their leaders were highly self-confident.

Perhaps to the disappointment of the DA, lack of honesty was not about finding leaders with their hands in the till or in other improper places. Expectations of honesty were much higher than that.

❝ The followers all wanted leaders they could trust. ❞

The followers all wanted leaders they could trust. Put simply, they could not trust a leader who was less than totally honest with them. This strong-form honesty (having the courage to tell the truth even when it is painful) was more than the mere absence of lying. Examples of strong-form honesty included:

▶ Being open about performance problems. A person who is not performing wants to know early enough to do something about it. They do not want a nasty surprise in the form of zero annual bonus.

▶ Sharing information. If the CEO suddenly cancels all meetings for a week and disappears into closed meetings with advisors, people get nervous. They want to know what is happening.

▶ Admitting mistakes. Followers hate it when the CEO lets shit run downhill; it creates a blame culture. Everyone passes the buck. It stops the organization from recognizing and rectifying mistakes before they do too much damage.

Strong-form honesty takes both courage and self-confidence. But if a leader wants to have followers, followers have to trust the leader. If they do not trust the leader, they will not follow.

At this point, the honesty challenge disappears off the optional ethics course at business school. It becomes part of the mandatory survival course for leaders.

Humility

Humble leadership brings us back to the curious world of the oxymoron. All the leaders used the word in the same way. They did not mean that the leader had to drive a second-hand car, wear old clothes and do menial jobs to set an example. They meant that the leader had to have acute self-awareness.

Good leaders need to know what they don't know. They need to recognize their limitations and to recognize their weaknesses and errors. Once a leader has the self-awareness and self-confidence to do this, a series of benefits flows:

▶ The leader can build an effective leadership team which complements their own strengths and weaknesses. Arrogant leaders believe that they can do it all themselves; this puts an impossible burden on them. Groups have greater wisdom than individuals. In 'Who Wants to Be a Millionaire' the phone-a-friend option gives the right answer 67% of the time. The option of asking the audience of amateurs and unknown strangers yields the right answer 91% of the time.

There is an old Chinese saying: 'The person who is right half the time is clever. The person who is right three-quarters of the time is clever and lucky. The person who is right all the time is a fool.' The humble leader is not so foolish as to believe they are infallible. They build their teams, not their egos.

▶ The leader can rectify errors fast, before they cause too much damage. Having the humility to recognize mistakes and act on them is essential.

▶ The leader creates a positive environment for progress. The infallible leader will naturally blame set-backs on ineffective staff and managers, who then all play the game of pass the parcel. This parcel of blame has the habit of exploding when the music stops. No one wants to take responsibility; fingers start to be pointed at each other; politics and the blame game take over. Fixing the underlying problem plays second fiddle to allocating blame.

Alternative styles of leadership

Much has been written about different leadership styles. The essence of this book is that each leader creates a unique leadership DNA based on begging and borrowing bits of leadership DNA from all the other leaders and role models they have observed over the years. All this book does is to help you accelerate your journey of discovery by helping you observe and reflect on the different ways in which leaders can succeed. If you are thinking that this is just a long apology for not giving you the single, brilliant theory of leadership which will transform your life, you are right.

Having made my apologies, it is possible to identify four and a half broad types of leadership. Most leaders sway between all of the four major types of leadership. A few leaders focus exclusively on the half type of leadership.

Here are the four-and-a-half types of leadership:

1 Autocrat

2 Bureaucrat/technocrat

3 Aristocrat

4 Democrat/meritocrat

4½ Kleptocrat.

Take a quick look at the summary below. Decide where you are and where your peers and bosses are.

	Key driver	Preferrred habitat	Strengths	Kryptonite/ weaknesses
Autocrat	Success, achievement, recognition	Entrepreneurs, crises	Decision making, drive	Scale, complexity, succession
Bureaucrat/ technocrat	Control, accuracy, perfection	Large, complex organizations	Fair, thorough, safe pair of hands, good process	Rapid change, uncertainty
Aristocrat	Title, status	Any non- executive role	Won't rock the boat, pliable	Harmless verging on useless
Democrat/ meritocrat	Excellence, performance	Wherever the other tyrannies are absent	Flexible, balanced, progressive	Needs right habitat to survive
Kleptocrat	Money, perks, privileges	Where's the money?	Money	Disaster for everyone else

Let us deal with each of them. Hold your nose while we dispense quickly with the half type of leadership: the kleptocrat.

The kleptocrat

The great kleptocracies of the world are alive and kicking. They are as destructive of businesses as they are of nations, and they share many similar traits. In both cases a small elite engineers a takeover from the inside and proceeds to treat the assets of the business or the nation as their own. During the dot.com boom 25 executives from six of the most spectacular bankruptcies awarded themselves a cool $2.6 billion for their collective failure. That is over $100 million each as a bounty for bankrupting their businesses and wasting other people's money.

The kleptocratic tendency exists in milder form in many organizations. The golden hellos and golden parachutes, the performance-linked bonus which is virtually guaranteed, the re-priced options, the perks and privileges of office are all hugely tempting. If they are clearly seen to be earned and deserved, most people do not begrudge them. When it is seen to be riding the gravy train of entitlement and privilege, it erodes trust and respect. The leader lands up looking the wrong way – at their bank account, not at their organization.

Two specious reasons are given for the explosion of CEO pay. One is that this rare talent may get poached. Few CEOs get poached; most are fired and then disappear into the obscurity of a few non-executive roles and government commissions. The other reason is the benchmark escalator. The escalator works like this:

▶ The compensation consultants show what average pay is for the top job.

▶ The board naturally believes their new CEO must be above average, so they pay above average.

▶ The compensation consultants now find their average has moved up, so they tell all the other boards, who adjust pay upwards in a never ending spiral.

As an alternative, it would be interesting to see what would happen if budding CEOs had to bid for their positions as suppliers of labour. They would probably offer a bid focused much more on performance and on rewards genuinely linked to delivering the promised performance.

It is easy to express moral outrage, tinged with a little envy, at the antics of the kleptocrats. As leaders, we have a decision to make about how we want to be remembered. As followers, we have a decision about who we are prepared to work for.

> ❝ *As leaders, we have a decision to make about how we want to be remembered.* ❞

The autocrat

The autocrat can do great things and good things. They can also be a disaster. The autocrat is often held up as the ideal model of leadership. The autocrat is seen as the all-powerful, all-wise leader who single-handedly leads an organization to the promised land. This is a popular media myth: it is much easier to write about colourful personalities doing flamboyant things than it is to talk about a leadership team quietly working to make an organization succeed.

Most entrepreneurs are instinctive autocrats. Because they have a deep passion for their creation, they understand it inside out. They want to keep on top of every detail. They have a track record which tells them that they have a successful way of leading. Most entrepreneurs are familiar with the following routine:

- ▶ When they start out they are told that they are bound to fail and what they are trying to do is impossible.
- ▶ As they start to succeed, all sorts of hangers-on try climbing on board and claiming a slice of the action.
- ▶ After they have succeeded, everyone tells them that they got lucky.

Given this experience, successful entrepreneurs have a right to feel a little superior and to trust their judgement more than those of all the experts and hangers-on. Within more established organizations, people who have succeeded against the odds often have the same tendency. And some people are just plain arrogant and bossy.

The autocratic form of leadership works where the organization is small enough that one person can get their hands and their intellect around it. It also works where the organization is in crisis and needs fast decisions.

Autocracy fails in the face of complexity and size. The autocrat finds it difficult to build an effective leadership team. There is simply no one else who comes up to the standards of wisdom, performance, enthusiasm and excellence that autocrats believe they have. And yet the organization becomes too big for one person to manage. Slowly, the autocrat loses touch, loses control and the business spins off the track. Some entrepreneurs get around this by moving to a conglomerate style of business. They manage by numbers, results and often by fear – make the numbers, or else. The autocracy simply gets replicated throughout the conglomerate.

Autocratic leaders also typically fail to build strong teams or strong succession. Because the autocrat controls everything personally, followers are not entrusted to make decisions and to lead themselves. They do not get the opportunity to develop their skills; they do not get leadership experience. When the great leader leaves, there is a vacuum. Naturally, this confirms the opinion of the autocrat that they were the only person capable of leading the organization; no one has been able to fill the autocrat's boots. This failure is the lasting legacy of the autocrat. The autocrat is the last person to recognize they caused the failure.

The bureaucrat/technocrat

The bureaucrat is much maligned, and sometimes rightly so. A good bureaucratic machine is one that manages huge complexity fairly and efficiently. It is something of a technocracy – a rational world where rational decisions are made under the twin guiding stars of efficiency and fairness.

The technocratic leader is often quite self-effacing. They recognize that success lies with the strength of the machine they run, not with the operator of the machine. They are often hugely trustworthy people. They typically care more about fair and efficient processes than about achieving great outcomes.

As leaders, the technocrats are good at maintaining and enhancing a legacy. Do not look to the technocrat to create a new legacy. Rapid change, uncertainty, risk and ambiguity are like kryptonite to them. They are not comfortable in start-ups or in rapidly evolving crises. They are more comfortable in the public sector and the more stable, traditional industries like retail banking and insurance.

The technocrats will never change the world, but they will probably run the world before and after it has been changed.

The aristocrat

Aristocratic and wannabe aristocrats are everywhere. Try asking someone what they do. If they reply, 'I am a partner/vice president/senior manager/director at . . .', they are not telling you what they do. They are telling you about their title and position. This is what is important to them. Work and achievement are unfortunate, grubby barriers they have to jump on the way to title and status. You will see young wannabe aristos proudly displaying their gold cards from airlines. They will happen to drop into conversation that they have just got back from LA/shooting/fishing/skiing/the Grand Prix/meeting the president. One such wannabe exploded with anger when I made fun of his platinum card from BA: he had wrapped his whole meaning into flying first class frequently. It made him feel important. In practice, he was going to irrelevant internal meetings at huge expense to feed his ego. The platinum card was a measure of just how much money he had wasted.

The ultimate goal of the aristocrat is the non-executive position, or chairing a government commission with a view to getting a knighthood. Both roles give prestige but require no responsibility. In their quest for status, the aristocrats become very pliable. They will find what the government wants them to find on the commission; they will nod through the CEO's outrageous compensation package. There is no need to bribe them. They are so hungry for status they happily corrupt their judgement for you.

The best that can be said of the aristocrats is that they are largely harmless. Like the French aristocracy before the revolution they are also largely useless. They gently corrode the values of their organization; they represent the triumph of froth over substance and create an 'us versus them' culture. The aristo turns left on entering the plane; the proles turn right; they have separate lifts, dining rooms and parking spaces. It is a class system which undermines the whole organization.

Many good leaders are narrowband leaders: they succeed in one context. Success goes to their heads. They believe in their own greatness. They get invited to sit on boards where they know nothing of the business or the organization in the mistaken belief that their narrowband success can be replicated everywhere else by turning up on one or two days a month. Narrowband leaders need to stick to what they are good at. The temptation to go broadband, to join the aristocracy, is overwhelming. Few resist this final twist to their careers.

The democrat/meritocrat

A democratic leader sounds like a weak leader. But try telling Pericles, Washington, Lincoln, Churchill or Thatcher that they were either weak or not democratic. History shows that democracy thrives where the other tyrannies can be defeated or avoided. History also shows that democracy is advancing. As people become wealthier and better educated, they have more choice and they expect to have more say in whatever affects their lives.

The democratic leader has to combine three qualities:

▶ Ability. The leader needs to have a proven track record.

▶ Support. The leader needs to be recognized, trusted and supported by peers.

▶ Circumstance. History is littered with nearly-leaders. They might have been great, but the conditions were wrong. Even Churchill suffered his 'wilderness years': it was war that made him.

The democratic leader will try to balance the need for excellence and fairness (the bureaucrat) with the need for decisiveness and speed (the autocrat). They will try to build commitment through inclusiveness and consultation. But they will balance that with the need for clarity, responsibility and accountability. They discover that there is no simple formula for leadership. Instead, there are endless trade-offs and balancing acts that need to be managed daily.

Many democratic leaders are narrowband leaders. They succeed in one particular industry, organization or set of circumstances. The leader who has made their career building the top line will not know how to react when there is a bottom-line crisis that requires radical cost surgery. Great bankers do not make great retailers. This creates a challenge for the board as it seeks a new CEO. The new CEO is not just a leader. Each candidate is a different solution in search of a problem. The finance-focused candidate will not suddenly be transformed into the customer champion when entering the CEO's office. The board has to know what problem they are trying to solve before they look at any candidates.

So what?

By the time the leader emerges from the middle of the organization into the top leadership position, the die is already cast. The leader has developed a set of skills and a style that will not change. In Shakespeare's words:

'There's a divinity that shapes our ends,
Rough-hew them how we will.'

— Hamlet *V, ii*

From this point on, the leader's career follows Shakespeare's plays. It turns out to be tragedy or comedy before becoming history. All leaders hope that their script is *All's Well That Ends Well*.

If the die is cast before the leader emerges at the top, there are two major implications.

The first is that the emerging leader needs to manage their values and their style from an early stage in their career. Early role models are decisive. It is natural to copy someone who is successful. This book says that there are many different ways in which you can succeed. You have a choice to make about the sort of person and the sort of leader you want to become. You need to be aware of that choice all the time, rather than blindly following role models. Most people do not make a conscious decision about who they want to be as a leader – they drift into a style. Sometimes they are lucky, sometimes they are unlucky. This book gives you a choice.

The second implication is that the established leader can have a huge impact on future generations of leadership. Emerging leaders watch you: they see what you do, who you reward and why and how you work. Your legacy is not just the business you leave behind, it is the values you leave behind.

Creating values for the organization at large

Leaders create a legacy which future generations of leaders can build on and enhance. Part of the legacy comes in the form of results – the size, scope and strength of the organization. Another part of the leader's legacy is the values that are left behind. These are likely to last longer than the results the leader achieved. Anyone who has been through a merger will recognize how long it takes for values and cultures to change. Even ten years after the event, individuals will identify each other as coming from side A or side B; the merged group C is simply a veneer that is applied to the underlying cultures of the two old organizations.

66 Leaders create a legacy which future generations of leaders can build on and enhance. 99

In this section we will look at the what and the how of creating effective values. We will start with looking at what common values are effective and ineffective.

Look at the values statement from one company in the box below. But don't look too long. It is tedious and irritating in equal proportions. It is a typical agglomeration of worthy words. In essence, their values aspire to sainthood. If you can identify the company or the industry in which it operates, you are doing very well. In fairness to them, their values statement is neither worse nor better than much of the drivel that passes as values statements in other organizations.

Typical values statement

Delivering on our mission
The tenets central to accomplishing our mission stem from our core company values:

A global, inclusive approach
Thinking and acting globally, enabling a diverse workforce that generates innovative decision making for a broad spectrum of customers and partners, and showing leadership in supporting the communities in which we work and live.

Excellence
In everything we do.

Trustworthy
Deepening customer trust through the quality of our products and services, our responsiveness and accountability, and our predictability in everything we do.

Great people with great values
Delivering on our mission requires great people who are bright, creative, and energetic, and who share the following values:

- ▶ Integrity and honesty.
- ▶ Passion for customers, partners, and technology.
- ▶ Open and respectful with others and dedicated to making them better.
- ▶ Willingness to take on big challenges and see them through.
- ▶ Self-critical, questioning, and committed to personal excellence and self-improvement.
- ▶ Accountable for commitments, results, and quality to customers, shareholders, partners, and employees.

A good values statement will achieve the following:

- ▶ Everyone can remember it. If people can't remember the values, they can't act on them. Twelve words maximum.

- ▶ It helps staff decide what to do in ambiguous situations. Do I give a refund or make margin? Do I confront improper behaviour or let it go?

- ▶ It relates to the particular needs of that organization – customer service, attention to detail, fairness, innovation, whatever.

- ▶ It lasts. Values, like dogs, are not just for Christmas.

- ▶ It is enforceable and actionable. Thinking globally is tough for a cleaner.

Values, like dogs, are not just for Christmas.

Using the criteria above, try scoring the values satement opposite.

Now contrast the very sophisticated values statement with the values of Timpson's chain of shoe repair shops. John Timpson, the owner of the shops, has not crafted a values statement to put on bronze plaques. Instead, he has created a picture with a series of Mr Men on it. He has pictures of the nine Mr Men he wants to employ in his shops: Mr Happy, Mr Friendly, Mr Keen, Mr Faithful, Mr Prompt, Mr Reliable, Mr Neat, Mr Smart and Mr Skilful.

Just as important, he created another set of Mr Men pictures for the people he does not want: Mr Can't Do, Mr Messy, Mr Dishonest, Mr Dull, Mr Grumpy, Mr Lazy, Mr Fib, Mr Late and Mr Dirty.

OK – he is not doing too well on diversity. But the pictures give a very clear idea to all the staff about how they are meant to behave and how they are not meant to behave. They do not have to be saints; these are values they can live up to. They are the sorts of behaviours that a customer would be happy to find in a shoe repair shop. It also gives a very clear idea to the area managers who they should be recruiting. They do not look for skilled cobblers because they can train for those skills. They are looking for a very distinctive set of behaviours. These are values that are relevant, sustainable, actionable and memorable.

Great care needs to be taken in building the right values for an organization. There are many popular buzz words that are thoughtlessly included in values statements. Passion is very much flavour of the month – pizza boys are meant to be passionate about pizza and cleaners are meant to be passionate about toilet bowls. It is relatively easy for the founder or leader of an organization to feel passionate about their 'baby'. They should avoid projecting their own passion on to everyone else. Demanding passion as one executive did – 'I want to see our logo emblazoned on the hearts of all our staff' – is not helpful. The same executive then wondered why they employed a majority of women, but none made it to the executive suite. Not everyone wants to become a fully signed-up member of a cult: some have lives outside work as well.

Making the values real

You have the values statement. You have the bronze plaques and motivational posters to go with it. You have even recorded a piece on camera for the annual convention and for all new-hire inductions. Nothing happens. All those hours spent arguing over the nuances of each carefully crafted word has come to nothing.

A large ocean separates the hope of the official values from the reality of the unofficial values within the organization. There are two steps to bridging the gap between hope and reality: communications and action.

Communicating the values

Endless communication of the values is an essential, but exhausting, part of building the values of the organization. It is also very dangerous.

You have just come up with some great new values for the organization. You want to embed a new set of behaviours to carry the organization forwards. You get on stage, wave your arms and enthusiastically communicate the new vision. The response sounds nearer to mutiny than adoration. What went wrong?

To tell people you are going to change the culture of the organization is toxic:

▶ Cultural revolutions do not have a good history. Think Mao and tens of millions of deaths.

▶ Telling people you are going to change the culture is like telling them that you are going to mess with their heads and change the way they think and behave. Not everyone gets excited about this.

▶ Changing values is an implicit attack on the past. It is like saying the way you have been behaving is no good. Not many people like to be told they have spent the last 20 years getting it wrong.

▶ The brave new world sounds exciting to you, but dangerous to them. Can they succeed in this alien world you have described?

If you want to build a new culture, do not attack the old one. It simply invites a battle. Instead, act like a crab; tackle the culture sideways on. Continue to celebrate and reinforce those parts of the old culture that are still useful; emphasize one or two new things that will be important in the future; ignore and let wither some of the old values that are less useful.

> **❝ If you want to build a new culture, do not attack the old one. It simply invites a battle. ❞**

Once you have the right message you will find yourself having to communicate it endlessly, and for years. It will need constant repetition through all the media. It is a war of attrition. But even more than your words, people will believe your actions.

Enacting the values

In practice, followers learn the right and wrong sorts of behaviour from three vital influences:

1 Pay, performance and promotion systems
2 Tough decisions
3 Personal behaviour of the CEO and symbolic acts

Pay, performance and promotion systems

In many organizations, these are still not properly aligned with the values or objectives of the organization. The telecommunications company trumpets customer service, but rewards its call centre staff on the number of calls they process. The result: incomplete and dropped calls, and hurried customers as the call centre staff try to meet their hourly call targets. A consulting company values professional integrity and team work. It promoted to partner the manager who had acquired some big accounts. The manager had also tested the limits of the expense system and been highly political. Everyone understood the real rules – sell big or die.

The pay and promotion systems are the acid test of the values a leader really believes in.

Tough decisions

The school head decided, with the staff, that respect for the individual was going to be the central value of the school. The staff had some idea what this might mean, but no one was really sure.

One day, a teacher mentioned that they were going to give a class detention to the sixth year. There had been some cheating, and the teacher wanted to make the point that cheating was unacceptable. The head teacher was horrified. You cannot give group detentions to the guilty and innocent alike; you have to respect the individual. The teacher had to go back and do more work to separate the guilty and innocent.

The PE teacher in the same school was a traditionalist who believed everyone should aspire to high standards of fitness. If you did not have high standards and ability, you suffered. The teacher seemed to believe in ritual humiliation of the fat, unfit and asthmatic. The head teacher observed that this did not amount to respect for the individual. The PE teacher could either change or change schools. He changed schools.

The staff learned what 'respect for the individual' meant not through speeches, but through practical, hard decisions. As a leader, you need to think through the logical consequences of the fine words you talk about, and then see those consequences through to their conclusion.

Personal behaviour of the CEO and symbolic acts

New CEOs are often surprised to find out how much power they really have. They expected and understood the nature of the formal authority they would inherit. They are often more surprised by the informal authority they have. People take their cues from the leader, who is the ultimate role model. One leader of an organization which employed many low paid staff realized he needed to cut costs dramatically to meet profit targets. He announced the plan at a company meeting of area and regional managers. He told them to beware of tough decisions on pay and redundancies. Everyone would have to make sacrifices. He had personally ordered the air conditioning in the board room to be turned off. This all sounded great. He left the event in his chauffeur-driven Bentley to attend a big corporate hospitality event. He lost all credibility with his managers and was later fired.

Another CEO decided he wanted to create a more open culture. He announced a new open-door policy. He had an open door, but it was on the thirteenth floor, accessible only through the special executive lift. He knew the thirteenth floor was referred to as death row by staff. They were summoned there sometimes to be promoted, but more staff were summoned there to get fired.

The CEO realized that an open door behind a closed elevator made little sense. He decided he should show that he was more open. He summoned up his courage and went to the alien world of the seventh floor. Staff were in shock. They had never seen a director, let alone the previous CEO. They all made themselves busy and tried to avoid eye contact. Eventually, the CEO found one unlucky clerk to talk to. There was nowhere for him to sit. Instinctively, he took an empty waste basket, turned it upside down and sat on it to get down to the level of the clerk. They talked about nothing very much. But news of the revolution spread like wildfire: he was a boss who anyone could actually talk to.

Being asked to walk the talk on values is irritating and unhelpful. It is not really clear what you are meant to do or how you are meant to do it. In practice, you can walk the talk if you focus on the three basic ideas outlined above.

PART FOUR

The leadership journey

12

The leadership journey and the three and a half *P*s of leadership

We have travelled on a long leadership journey. Along the way we have visited the many skills and behaviours that can be learned and which form the tool kit of a successful leader.

But something is missing. All the leaders I interviewed focused on being positive, professional and people orientated. But only one leader really focused on the remaining *P*: performance. Others mentioned performance in passing, but it was never a real focus of the discussion.

Leadership without performance is a curious concept. The evidence from top leaders is that performance expectations are getting higher and tolerance of failure is getting lower. The career expectancy of a FTSE-100 CEO is now under five years. All political careers are said to end in ultimate failure. Business seems to be heading in the same direction.

There are at least four possible reasons why most of our leaders did not focus on performance as a key issue:

▶ Performance may be as natural for leaders as breathing air. You do not need to remind people of the need to breathe when they wake up in the morning.

▶ They may believe that performance is a natural result of being positive, professional and people focused in the right way.

▶ Performance may mean such different things in different sorts of organizations that they felt it was difficult to abstract any principles about the nature of performance.

▶ Performance may not have been important to them in defining an effective leader.

For all these reasons we cannot make performance the fourth *P* of the leadership journey. We can at most make it a half *P*. So we now have the three-and-a-half *P*s theory of leadership. This potentially breaks every rule of business theory. Business theory comes in whole numbers:

▶ one core competence and strategic intent

▶ any two by two matrix you care to invent

▶ three *C*s of marketing (customers, channels and competition – marketers do not worry about costs)

▶ four *P*s of marketing, just to confuse you (product, price, promotion, place)

▶ management in fives (Mintzberg)

▶ six sigma quality

▶ seven *S*s (McKinsey). No, I can't remember them either.

But three *and a half*? Let's call it innovation.

Performance and the leadership journey

Performance echoes the rest of the leadership journey. It means different things at different levels of the organization, and it means different things in different organizations. It is context specific.

❝ Performance means different things at different levels of the organization, and it means different things in different organizations. ❞

However, there are some common characteristics of the performance expected of actual and potential leaders at each level of the organization.

Performance for emerging leaders: learning to lead

Performance criteria for emerging leaders tend to be fairly clear. There is not a lot of discretion in defining what good performance looks like; others do the defining for you. The expectations may be high and demanding, but they are at least clear.

Performing well against target is not enough to be a good leader. The best sports person is not necessarily the best team captain or coach. Technical excellence is not a predictor of leadership excellence.

To the extent that leaders could see potential leadership talent emerging, they were looking for more than just performance. They were looking at how the performance was achieved.

The following was typical of the view from the top:

'I expect people to learn about our organization, learn their trade and learn about themselves. I want them to immerse themselves in what we do. I do not need them to change the world as soon as they arrive. If they ask good questions and have self-confidence that is a good start. I want them to start working with other people, not just by themselves.'

In these simple comments lies a trap for aspiring leaders. The natural focus of anyone new to the working world is to want to perform. The way we have learned to perform throughout the education system is by working hard and by ourselves. Emerging leaders are not isolated individuals; they make things happen with and through other people. This takes a high degree of self-awareness. In the words of another of the leaders: 'Self-awareness is about knowing how your actions affect other people.' Self-awareness is not navel gazing and wondering what sort of a person you are. It is about how you engage with other people.

The view from the top shows why performance only merits half a point in the leadership stakes. Top leaders expect to see everyone perform well. But performance does not differentiate the future leaders of tomorrow from the rest. Take the best 20 footballers in any country, and perhaps only one of them will become a successful manager. Technical performance does not indicate leadership potential.

Performance in the middle

Middle management is the home of ambiguity. Even if the targets are clear, the resources required for achieving the targets are not clear.

Some excellent performers get lost in the middle. They rise from the ranks on the back of excellent technical performance in their chosen field. They have quietly developed a formula for personal success which is based on technical excellence. They soon find that this formula may get them off the plains and into the foothills, but it will never help them scale the peaks of leadership. They may, with great effort and stress, carry a whole department on the basis of their technical excellence in sales, trading, research or what-ever trade they have learned. But they cannot carry a whole organization on that basis. They have to figure out how to let go – how to help other people do things which they might like to do themselves. For these people, per-formance is a barrier to leadership, not a ladder to leadership.

Leaders cannot pass through the perils of middle management by themselves. They have to acquire the personal and political skills of working through other people and departments. The have to coach, motivate, make alliances, build networks and learn how to pull the power levers of the organization.

In the middle, performance and perception are closely related. Most leaders in the middle intuitively know the success formula:

$$Success = Performance - Expectations$$

They know that it makes sense to set expectations as low as possible. One month of hard bargaining over budget saves eleven months of trial and tribulation later. Before dismissing this as undue cynicism, watch what hap-pens when a new CEO is appointed. More often than not, they will clear all the skeletons out of the cupboards, make write-offs and set expectations low about the true nature of the business they have inherited. It is easier to perform against a low base than it is against a high base. CEOs do not learn this trick by accident on the day they are appointed; it is standard survival practice learned earlier in their careers.

Clearly, performance does count. You cannot rise to the top without some form of claim to fame. In the first instance you may be given a 'lemonade stand' to run – a small part of the organization where you can develop and demonstrate your leadership potential. But performance, politics and perception become closely entwined. For these reasons, performance in the middle merits at most half a point.

Performance at the top

Good performance and good leadership should be inseparable. And it should be clear what *good* means for the leader at the top. For public companies, there should be a clear focus on maximizing returns to the owners of the company, the shareholders. The short career expectancy of public company CEOs shows that many are found wanting when exposed to the chill winds of such clear expectations.

Except that nothing is quite so clear and simple. Different constituencies have completely different expectations of what a 'good' leader delivers. Customers, regulators, environmentalists and ethical campaigners all have quite different ideas. Maximizing shareholder returns does not appear on their agendas.

The leader's followers, the staff, do not see performance as a key attribute of the leader at all. Remember how they defined an effective leader:

- ability to motivate others
- vision
- honesty and integrity
- decisiveness
- ability to handle crises.

These characteristics are not about performance. They are not about good or evil. The great and evil dictators of the twentieth century, the men with moustaches, passed these five tests. They probably even passed the followers' definition of honesty: they consistently let people know where they stood (and shot them if it was in the wrong place).

We started with clarity and certainty; the good leader performs well. We have landed up shrouded in the fog of competing claims from different groups about what they expect from the leader. And performance does not even appear on the radar screen of followers. To followers, the only time performance becomes relevant is when the leader has to deliver on expectations about promotion, bonus or assignment. We have suddenly reached a post-modern end point of uncertainty and relativism about the nature of performance. It seems to mean different things to different people, and there is no absolute measure of good performance.

Fortunately, all the leaders we talked to and looked at did not suffer post-modern blues. They created simplicity and focus out of confusion and uncertainty. They created simple performance targets which everyone could understand and follow. Leaders who focus explicitly on shareholder value are the exception: Lloyds Bank in the 1980s and 1990s and Rentokil in the 1990s to the 2000s. Most focus on an intermediate target. Ryanair is focused on being the lowest-cost airline. It assumes that passenger growth targets and shareholder returns will be optimized by focusing on this intermediate target.

For an increasingly large part of the economy, profit is simply not a target at all. Part of the complexity of leadership in the NHS is that it does not really know what it is meant to achieve. There are thousands of targets and measures, but there is no single clear goal. There is still debate about the purpose of education: is it academic excellence, reducing social inequality and exclusion, preparing people for employment or embedding core social values?

Effective leaders at the top cut through this fog. They create certainty and focus where others suffer paralysis from an excess of choice. There is no perfectly correct choice.

The perfect is the enemy of the practical. A practical choice gives an organization focus and direction.

Given the pitfalls of defining what 'good' performance means for leadership, it is perhaps less surprising that our leaders focused more on skills and behaviours of successful leaders than on performance.

As with the other levels, we can, at most, we can give half a point to performance.

Completing the journey

Most books and gurus like to give you The Answer. Ideally, The Answer is simple. It will contain three points and can be summarized in a snappy phrase or acronym. You read the book, remember The Answer, and then you become a leader. Except, of course, that real life is not like that.

Life is becoming more complicated, more stressful and more time constrained. In this world we want quick, easy answers. So if anyone promises The Answer, it is very seductive. But once we have been let down a few times, our cynicism tends to grow about all such answers. We are left groping through the fog in search of leadership.

❝ The Answer in this book is that leadership is not a destination. It is a journey. ❞

Leadership is not some far distant objective that is all about a rare breed of human who controls the fate of nations and organizations. Leadership is here and now. We can all take part in the leadership journey. We may never lead the nation or a multinational organization. We can be leaders of a project team, a club, an expedition or a department. We can develop our leadership skills from the first day we start work.

Because most people focus on The Answer and the destination, they never focus on the journey.

Each person's journey is different. We all have different starting points, and we all have different leadership destinations. We will lead different types of organizations in different situations and with different styles. If the start and finish of a journey is different for each person, the journey in between will also be different.

For many people, the leadership journey is a random walk. Like a snakes and ladders game, we sometimes get in the right situation and rise rapidly; then we find ourselves working for a snake of a manager and fall rapidly back.

The journey does not have to be random. Although we cannot say 'turn left after six months and do this', we know that there are consistent sets of behaviours and skills which leaders tend to have. These skills and behaviours can be learned. They do not guarantee that anyone will become a leader or that they will become a heroic success as a leader. But they will load the dice heavily in favour of success.

We also know that leaders can exist at all levels of the organization. You do not have to wait to get the top job before you can demonstrate that you are a leader. In fact, you cannot afford to wait that long. Leaders practise and demonstrate their skills from a very early stage.

What this book has shown is that the expected skills and behaviours of the leader change at each level of the organization. These skills and behaviours are cumulative. In the past, people have talked vaguely of the importance of 'experience' for leaders. This does not help. It simply frustrates ambitious people by implying that they are going to have to wait thirty years before they can succeed. We have peeled away the mysteries of leadership to show what leaders need to do and what they need to learn, at each stage of their individual leadership journey.

With this road map to leadership, you do not have to become a heroic leader in the mould of the famous people that litter the pages of history books and business magazines. You cannot succeed by trying to be someone else. Equally, coasting along as yourself and hoping that the world will recognize your innate excellence will not work either. To succeed as a leader, you have to be the best of who you are. This book is not just a road map to being a leader. It is a road map to helping you become the best of who you are.

" *Whatever your journey is, enjoy it.* **"**

Further reading

Books

Bennis, Warren. (1989) *On Becoming a Leader*. Reading, Mass.: Addison-Wesley.

Carnegie, Dale. (1994) *How to Win Friends and Influence People*. London: Hutchison Books.

Collins, Jim. (2001) *Good to Great*. London: Random House Business Books.

Covey, S. (1992) *The Seven Habits of Highly Effective People*. London: Simon and Schuster.

Hesselbein, F. and Cohen, P. (eds). (1999) *Leader to Leader*. San Francisco: Josey Bass.

Kotter, John. (1988) *The Leadership Factor*. New York: Free Press.

Landsberg, Max. (2000) *The Tools of Leadership* London: HarperCollins.

Machiavelli, Niccolò. (1961) *The Prince*. London: Penguin Books.

Owen, Jo. (2002) *Management Stripped Bare*. London: Kogan Page.

Peters, T. and Waterman, R. (1982) *In Search of Excellence*. New York: Harper and Row.

Senge, Peter. (1992) *The Fifth Discipline*. London: Random House.

Timpson, John. (2002) *How to Be a Great Boss: The Timpson Way*. Timpson Ltd.

Wiseman, Richard. (2003) *The Luck Factor*. London: Arrow Books.

Harvard Business Review

Goleman, Daniel. What Makes an Effective Leader. Nov–Dec 1998.

Goleman, Daniel. Leadership That Gets Results. March–April 2000.

Kotter, John. What Effective General Managers Really Do. Jan 1999.

Kotter, John. What Leaders Really Do. April 1999.

Zaleznik, A., Mintzberg, H. and Gosling, J. Your Best Managers Lead and Manage. HBR OnPoint Collection. Jan 2003.

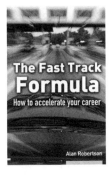

FT HANDBOOK OF MANAGEMENT

3rd edition
Edited by Stuart Crainer
0273 675842

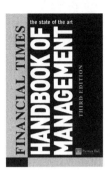

A world of management expertise delivered to your desktop in one single, definitive resource, this is THE classic business book for every executive's shelf.

Big ideas, brilliant minds and better ways; the *FT Handbook* is packed with intelligent writing to bring management alive for the thinking executive.

"Very large, very important and very comprehensive… indispensable"
The Bookseller

LIVING LEADERSHIP

A Practical Guide for Ordinary Heroes
George Binney
0273 693743

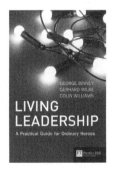

Based on a unique four-year experiment working alongside real leaders in real businesses, *Living Leadership* explodes the myth of the charismatic, transformational leader to show that real progress comes from the dramatically ordinary stuff of leadership. From building relationships - not starting revolutions, by working with the grain of your organisation not against it, and in knowing your limitations as much as pushing every boundary.

Living Leadership reveals a powerful set of principles and proven advice for managers who want to develop their leadership skills.

TOM PETERS – LIVE IN LONDON

Tom Peters
CD 0273 693972 Cassette 0273 693034

In these disruptive times, leadership is the hottest management topic. Listen to the world's leading management guru in one of his most powerful and inspiring seminars on leadership.

**A full range of Red Audio titles are available
from www.pearson-books.com/audio**

**If you wish to find out more about any of these titles or view our
full list visit us at: www.pearson-books.com**